The Saints

by Ron Crawford

PNEUMATIKOS PUBLISHING
P.O. 595351
Dallas, TX 75359

info@pneumatikos.com

© 2002 by Ron Crawford

Published by Pneumatikos Publishing
P.O. Box 593531
Dallas, TX 75359
E-Mail: info@pneumatikos.com
www.pneumatikos.com

First printing, September, 2002

Printed in the United States of America. All rights reserved under International Copyright Law. No part of this publication may be reproduced, stored in a retrieval system or transmitted in any form or by any means--for example, electronic, photocopy, recording—without the prior written permission of the publisher. The only exception is brief quotations for printed reviews.

ISBN #0-9720681-2-0

Morris Publishing
3212 E. Hwy 30
Kearney, NE 68847

Cover Art Work by Fabian Arroyo

Unless otherwise noted, scripture quotations are from the HOLY BIBLE, Authorized King James Version.

Table of Contents

Introduction	1
1 - Saintly Scriptures	5
2 - What Is a Saint?	17
3 - The Call To A Saints Movement	25
4 - Establishing The Kingdom	37
5 - Building Up The Saints	49
6 - A Graceful Conversion	69
7 - Becoming A Son Of God	79
8 - The Saintly Operation of Our Heavenly Father	85
9 - The Saintly Influence of The Holy Spirit	103
10 - The Lord Jesus in Saintly Development	111
11 - The Developmental Stages Of The Saints	127
12 - The Saints Of Righteousness	139
13 - The King Of Saints	167
14 - The Fine Linen Of The Saints	177
15 - Remembering The Love Of The Father	200

Preface

Following seven years as a staff member of Lakewood Assembly of God, Ron Crawford was elected Senior Pastor in 1987. I have had the privilege of serving beside Pastor Crawford as his associate pastor for the past 15 years.

Lakewood is a church with a very stable, long-tenured history that looked and acted like most of the church world until six years ago. At that time, our staff and church took a huge turn in direction. The major reason for this was a dynamic encounter we had with the Lord during a Pastor's Conference at Brownsville Assembly of God in Pensacola, Florida. Individually and corporately our lives were forever changed.

Pastor Crawford and I were immediately anointed with a burden to pray. We were both called to become intercessors for our church, our country and our world. I watched as God began activating and intensifying Pastor Crawford's spiritual gifts. He had moved in the prophetic and discernment before, but now greater dimensions of these giftings were evident, as God gradually began opening his eyes to the spirit realm.

Pastor Crawford had other options, but he chose the more difficult path. He chose to follow God, to pursue a daily, intimate, obedient relationship with our Heavenly Father – no matter what. He chose being a friend of God over friendships with congregation members who were very upset with his sudden passion for the heart of the Father. The result has been a remnant. Some in our congregation were quick to turn their hearts to God and have become powerful prayer warriors who live a life of holiness and dedication to God. At the same time, others rejected this all-out pursuit of God. He watched as his congregation dwindled to one-third of its original size because of his decision to serve God and not to be a man-pleaser.

Some would argue that God doesn't do things that way. I disagree. When you study the scriptures, you find case after case where God used a remnant of the people to accomplish His purposes. The Lord is looking for Gideons to lead His remnants into the higher places in God. Congregations made up of individuals who are tired of playing church have asked God to put to death their flesh and carnal nature, and to begin the transforming process of renewing their minds. These churches have made prayer and worship their top priority.

Pastor Crawford dared to go against the natural current of the church world today. He chose to obey God rather than men. He wholeheartedly accepted the call of God to move out of his comfort zone and become a leader in the army of God. Many powerful remnant congregations, filled with warriors for Christ, will lead the end-time move of God. These mighty men and women are known as **The Saints**.

Paul David Harrison

Introduction

Our world is embroiled in a cauldron of continual change and unsettledness. Troubling reports of terrorism and unrest fill the pages of our newspapers. International intrigue is dwarfed by the threat of insecurity in our once secure homeland. People are looking for peace in our time. There is something within the human framework that points us to the understanding that our answers can only be found in the realm of our spirit. Sadly, the dark realities of the demonic are actively recruiting for the purposes of Satan. An uncertain climate provides fertile soil for such conscription.

From well-staged and publicized books and films that pursue the imaginations of our little ones to independent television programs that target pre-teens, the youth of our country are prime targets for the army of darkness. Well-meaning but ignorant guardians are seemingly oblivious to the dangers of these enemy incursions. Blatant demonic propaganda is interpreted as harmless literary expression or modern day mythology.

The fact remains that this world is being prepared for war. The line of God's purpose has been drawn, and the sides are being chosen. The ultimate war for this planet will not be against a rogue nation or a militant belief system. Climactic conflict will occur between the forces of righteousness and unrighteousness. One will champion the purposes of God for the earth, and the other will rebelliously resist such innate truth.

The good news for the people of God is that the forces of righteousness will win a triumphant victory. The culmination of all things will result in a glorious victory for the forces of the Lord Jesus Christ. He is called the King of Saints in the Book of Revelation, and those that follow Him are a class of faithful warriors. They are the Saints.

Many prophetic voices within the church have spoken of the coming of such a group. In fact, some have gone so far as to label the coming move of God as the Saints Movement. God has spoken a vital and compelling truth into the hearts of His friends, the prophets. As usual, He has let them know the secrets of His heart. Like modern day voices that cry in the wilderness of our insensitivity and slumber, they declare the coming move of God.

The saints are the special forces of the armies of God. They are especially committed to the purposes of the Lord of Hosts. They form the corps of warriors that accompany the Lord Jesus Himself. In the days that are coming, the saints will actively confront the forces of darkness in open combat. Like Moses' encounter with the magicians of Pharaoh's court, the saints will forcefully display the overcoming power of God. Many nations will appeal to the saints for assistance in the days of trouble that will shortly burst upon the scene. The nations that enlist themselves in the service of the enemy will face the brunt of the curses and plagues of God that will be declared through the mouths of the saints in obedience to the Lord.

God will commit the full arsenal of His power and gifts to His saints. They will be equipped with strategies of warfare that will be brilliant in scope since they will be transcribed within the very heart of the Father in Heaven. The angels of the Lord will war alongside these mighty men and women as they champion the cause of God.

Are you ready for such a shift in the dynamic of the world? The days ahead will resemble nothing like any that mankind has ever known. To become a saint will require nothing less than total commitment to the purposes of the Father. The training for such intricate movement is occurring at this very hour. God is speaking to many that are called to such a mission. Scripture tells us that few are chosen. You can be one of the few, the humble, the Saints!

The Saints

Saintly Scriptures

Many of today's largest and most successful churches bear a resemblance to corporations or small cities more than the army of God. Their pastors resemble CEO's and mayors more than equippers of the Kingdom of God. There is much pressure to stay current and to find better modes of keeping the people happy and content. Pastoring a church in today's world has become more about managing than it is about pioneering. What a world!

I was one of those pastors for a very long time. Week after week I would preach sermons that were Biblically based but spiritually dormant. My people were happy with their lives and were content to be a part of our church life. However, very few showed any tangible sign of growth in the Lord, and there was a decided lack of excitement in serving God.

Knowing that there was something more than what I could see around me, I asked God to do whatever He wanted to do within me and in the church that He had called me to pastor. As a result of that request, many changes transpired and continue to evolve. Commune with God is now the watchword of our congregation, and we are more concerned with serving Him than with being served. This mindset created an environment wherein the Lord could begin to reveal His heart to us in many wondrous ways.

As an answer to prayer and fasting, God birthed a new work in our church. More importantly for me, He did it in my heart, too. He began to show me that there was much more to Him than just talking about Him, and He began to reveal Himself in intercession and in the study of His Word. God opened my eyes to the reality that there was more to being a follower of Him than simply holding on until the rapture.

One night as I was praying alone in my room, the Spirit of the Lord began to share some insights that were astounding. He revealed that there is a classification of believers that has been largely misunderstood and generally unknown to most of the church. Then the Lord opened my eyes to the existence of a people within the church that are extraordinary in relationship with Him and in importance to this world. These people are classified in the Bible as saints.

SAINTLY SCRIPTURES

Let us view a few of these passages.

1 Corinthians 1:2 Unto the church of God which is at Corinth, to them that are sanctified in Christ Jesus, called to be saints, with all that in every place call upon the name of Jesus Christ our Lord, both theirs and ours:

Ephesians 1:1 Paul, an apostle of Jesus Christ by the will of God, to the saints which are at Ephesus, and to the faithful in Christ Jesus:

Ephesians 2:19 Now therefore ye are no more strangers and foreigners, but fellowcitizens with the saints, and of the household of God;

Philippians 1:1 Paul and Timotheus, the servants of Jesus Christ, to all the saints in Christ Jesus which are at Philippi, with the bishops and deacons:

Colossians 1:2 To the saints and faithful brethren in Christ which are at Colosse: Grace be unto you, and peace, from God our Father and the Lord Jesus Christ.

2 Thessalonians 1:10 When he shall come to be glorified in his saints, and to be admired in all them that believe (because our testimony among you was believed) in that day.

Revelation 11:18 And the nations were angry, and thy wrath is come, and the time of the dead, that they should be judged, and that thou shouldest give reward unto thy servants the prophets, and to the saints, and them that fear thy name, small and great; and shouldest destroy them which destroy the earth.

Revelation 16:6 For they have shed the blood of saints and prophets, and thou hast given them blood to drink; for they are worthy.

Revelation 17:6 And I saw the woman drunken with the blood of the saints, and with the blood of the martyrs of Jesus: and when I saw her, I wondered with great admiration.

Revelation 18:24 And in her was found the blood of prophets, and of saints, and of all that were slain upon the earth.

Obviously there is a clear line of demarcation within the New Testament that designates the saints as being something different from other groupings of people within the general church. As I viewed this plethora of scriptures, as well as many other examples within the Word of God, I became hungry to discover the world of the saints.

There are additional passages within the Old Testament that give extraordinary reference to the people that are known as the saints. Within them, the saints are separated from the general reference to others within the tribes. Here are just a few examples of this powerful distinction within the Old Testament.

2 Chronicles 6:41 Now therefore arise, O Lord God, into thy resting place, thou, and the ark of thy strength: let thy priests, O Lord God, be clothed with salvation, and let thy saints rejoice in goodness.

Psalm 37:28 For the Lord loveth judgment, and forsaketh not his saints; they are preserved for ever: but the seed of the wicked shall be cut off.

Psalm 85:8 I will hear what God the Lord will speak: for he will speak peace unto his people, and to his saints: but let them not turn again to folly.

Psalm 89:7 God is greatly to be feared in the assembly of the saints, and to be had in reverence of all them that are about him.

Hosea 11:12 Ephraim compasseth me about with lies, and the house of Israel with deceit: but Judah yet ruleth with God, and is faithful with the saints.

Zechariah 14:5 ... and the Lord my God shall come, and all the saints with thee.

Let us turn our attention to the New Testament in order to learn of the way that the saints are identified within the New Covenant church.

THE GENERAL CHURCH

Classifications of people groups in the scripture are very specific and clear. The general church consists of many types of people, and within that body there are varied giftings and responsibilities. The general church must be valiant in itself, manifesting a passion for Christ and operating in the five-fold giftings defined in Ephesians 4.

Ephesians 4:11-12 And he gave some, apostles; and some, prophets; and some, evangelists; and some, pastors and teachers; 12 For the perfecting of the saints, for the work of the ministry, for the edifying of the body of Christ:

It is clear that the five-fold giftings that are given by the Lord Jesus are designed for the purpose of creating an atmosphere through which the saints are perfected. Not only are all five of these offices operational in this day, they are essential for the birthing of the purposes of God in this world. Without the correct alignment of these five, there can be no optimal climate of saintly development.

Ultimately we are to do the works of Christ. Simply stated, Jesus became the Christ as He accepted the anointing of the Holy Ghost in order to accomplish the purpose of the Heavenly Father. The apostle accepts the mandate of the Father and is sent forth. Prophets and teachers provide a sustained environment through which this type of transaction may occur. This is borne out in Acts 13 in the church at Antioch.

Acts 13:1-3 Now there were in the church that was at Antioch certain prophets and teachers; as Barnabas, and Simeon that was called Niger, and Lucius of Cyrene, and Manaen, which had been brought up with Herod the tetrarch, and Saul. 2 As they ministered to the Lord, and fasted, the

> Holy Ghost said, Separate me Barnabas and Saul for the work whereunto I have called them. 3 And when they had fasted and prayed, and laid their hands on them, they sent them away.

This progression is aptly depicted in Paul's writing to the church at Corinth.

> **1 Corinthians 12:28** And God hath set some in the church, first apostles, secondarily prophets, thirdly teachers...

The modern day prophets and teachers are very similar to the ministry of the prophet and seer in the Old Testament. The teacher/seer will grasp a spectrum of what God is saying and doing. The prophet will glean and declare a direct judgment of what the seer/teacher is depicting. Apostles will serve as the flagship gifting of this message bearing it forth into the places directed by the Spirit of God.

Evangelists will accomplish exploits on behalf of the Kingdom and will be rooted within the church. They will engage in divine appointments that often will have international implication. Remember that Philip the Evangelist, who was famous for signs, wonders and mighty deeds, was part of the local church. His household was known for prophetic gifting.

> **Acts 21:8-9** And the next day we that were of Paul's company departed, and came unto

Caesarea: and we entered into the house of Philip the evangelist, which was one of the seven; and abode with him. 9 And the same man had four daughters, virgins, which did prophesy.

Within the five-fold giftings of the church, pastors are responsible before God to maintain order and coordination within the Body. Undoubtedly they are the ones that preside over the flow of the **spiritual ones** or *pneumatikos*. The *pneumatikos* exists within the church as a representative unit of priests of the Heavenly Father[1].

WHEN DID THE FIVE-FOLD MINISTRY END?

Much of the established church has asserted that the five-fold ministry does not exist any longer. Pastors, teachers and evangelists are still acceptable entities within the body of Christ. Somehow lost within the paradigm of their doctrine are the important offices of apostle and prophet. Let us take a look at God's timetable concerning the existence of all of these offices.

> **Ephesians 4:12-13** For the perfecting of the saints, for the work of the ministry, for the edifying of the body of Christ: 13 Till we all come in the unity of the faith, and of the knowledge of

---

[1] For more information regarding this topic: *Pneumatikos* by Ron Crawford, Pneumatikos Publishing

> the Son of God, unto a perfect man, unto the measure of the stature of the fulness of Christ:

The last time I checked, we were not fulfilling the mandate of Verse 13. In point of truth, we are a very long way from fulfilling that lofty status. Therefore, since the verse begins with "Till," it would be logical to assert that all five of these offices must exist "till" we are promoted into that place of maturity in God.

We need these offices to be in operation so that the saints can continue to be perfected in their development and service to God. It is no wonder that an understanding of the saints is lacking within the church. As the five-fold ministry is essential for the development of the saints, it stands to reason that a church bereft of these offices would also be bereft of saintly ministry.

When the saints are fully active, the work of ministry will broaden and expand to accomplish the full counsel of God. The body of Christ will manifest the anointing of God according to His calling and purpose. According to the preceding scripture, the five-fold ministry will yield an understanding of what God is doing on earth as well as develop and equip an anointed group of saints. This will usher in a fullness wherein the works of Christ will be witnessed in abundance.

Those who will do exploits for the advancement of the Kingdom of God in righteousness must flow through this general body. Saints will arise from the midst of the general church, and they will be a special forces unit of the Kingdom. They will receive revelation of fresh mysteries, battle in the heavenlies, and do the bidding of the Father on an unprecedented scale.

Hidden within the Bible is the framework for the next mighty move of God – the marching order for the armies that will battle the antichrist in what will be the final thrust of God on this planet before the millennial reign. God is formulating and training this army right now, and He is promoting men and women to be leaders in that army. God needs people, and He is looking at you.

It is God's time for the saints to arise. Are you one of them?

The Saints

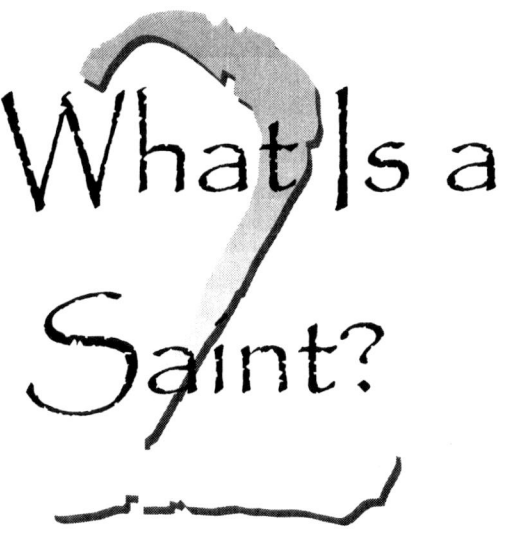

Like a thief in the night the progression of God's revelation is flowing amidst a general church that is slumbering. God has called His people to a dimension of service in these final hours. The designation of this calling has been titled "Saints," and this movement is already in motion within the body of Christ.

The saints were portrayed in the early church as people at the forefront during that dispensation of revelation. This prototype established the realm of what a saint is supposed to be today: those who dwell in the vanguard of what God is doing in our world. God is continually recruiting. He calls many but finds few.

TRADITIONAL INTERPRETATION

In the western mindset the name "saint" connotes many abstract and vague definitions. To some the title could evoke the thought of a football team; to others a lively jazz tune. Some may picture a halo-ed loved one, a Godly servant who is very humble, or a stalwart soul that has made it through this life to an eternal reward.

For western ideology the name "saint" is simply an interchangeable name for a Christian. All of these mindsets serve to cloak or dilute the true vitality of what a saint really is supposed to accomplish in and before the Lord.

WHAT IS A SAINT?

Much of the ideology of sainthood was developed during the past two thousand years within the Roman Catholic Church. The remaining viewpoint has been crystallized into a set of official guidelines for how Rome recognizes a saint. Sainthood classes are offered at the Vatican for would-be saints or for those who want to champion the cause of those that are no longer among us in a physical sense. Simply stated, a "saint" is a pious individual that has died and gone on to be with God. To separate themselves from the designation of those who simply have expended their appointed time on earth, this departed saint would need to have known the power of God to the degree that their earthly existence patterned a heroic lifestyle of faith and virtue.

In order to be officially recognized by Rome as being a saint, a stringent order of application must be followed. This includes, but is not limited to, a mountainous process of detailed research into the deceased person's life. This research must then be submitted in the form of a position, a document resembling a doctoral thesis. After the thesis is submitted, it may be accepted for review by a large group of Cardinals and Bishops who comprise a "Congregation for the Causes of the Saints."

If the person in review is deemed worthy, the group and the Pope confer a title of "Venerable." This title ends the matter of reviewing their life while among the living. Then comes the issue of posthumous miracles. If the "venerable" can be attributed by credible witnesses to have transacted one posthumous miracle, they are conferred the title "Blessed." Upon performing two verifiable posthumous miracles, they become a "Saint." Much deliberation and championing of the cause is required as well as a great deal of work mixed with an extraordinary dollop of unquestioned faith in the concept and plan.

While Protestant thinking may rightfully scoff at this process, their own viewpoints regarding saintly ministry are in many ways more skewed. At least the Catholics believe that saints are different from regular folk in the way of pious existence and grand deeds before God. Is that markedly errant in comparison to a viewpoint that dilutes saintly duty to general status? The point for us is that the enemy has successfully cloaked the existence of this unique group of people. In that light, few believe that God has classified a group of saints that are different from the general church. Subsequently, the exploits that would be flowing through this class of believers lie dormant. When you see the truth of the Word and believe, nothing will be called impossible. If you do not know what God says, you will not step into His dimension of might and power.

As opposed to the doctrines of man, there is a specific Biblical process toward becoming a saint that is regulated and empowered by the Holy Ghost. As a special forces unit within the Body of Christ, the saints will be doing the main battling against the forces of darkness in the end-time. Look at this sampling of scripture taken from the Book of Daniel.

> **Daniel 7:18** But the saints of the most High shall take the kingdom, and possess the kingdom for ever, even for ever and ever.
>
> **Daniel 7:2** And the kingdom and dominion, and the greatness of the kingdom under the whole heaven, shall be given to the people of the saints of the most High, whose kingdom is an everlasting kingdom, and all dominions shall serve and obey him.
>
> **Jude 1** And Enoch also, the seventh from Adam, prophesied of these, saying, Behold, the Lord cometh with ten thousands of his saints.

God is in the process of mobilizing this corps of passionate warriors. This has been prophesied as a present truth revelation by a multitude of credible prophetic voices. Some leaders have spoken of how God will use the saints in incredibly dynamic points of ministry. Until this time the cost of attaining this heady dimension of existence has been vague.

CAN WE HANDLE THIS?

From personal observation the general church as it is today will not tolerate this information in an agreeable manner. The general church will resent the implication and teaching that there is something more required of them than what they already have achieved. The general church will talk of Christ's victory and how because of it we do not need to fight anything other than our own vices. It is much easier to speak of platitudes of grandeur in the Word than to actually pay the price required to live within them.

FIG TREES AND THE MODERN CHURCH

> **Mark 11:13-14** And seeing a fig tree afar off having leaves, he came, if haply he might find any thing thereon: and when he came to it, he found nothing but leaves; for the time of figs was not yet. 14 And Jesus answered and said unto it, No man eat fruit of thee hereafter for ever. And his disciples heard it.

> **Mark 11:20-21** And in the morning, as they passed by, they saw the fig tree dried up from the roots. 21 And Peter calling to remembrance saith unto him, Master, behold, the fig tree which thou cursedst is withered away.

This episode with the fig tree used to trouble me. I would often read this scripture with an unspoken perception that perhaps Jesus was displaying an improper attitude toward the poor little fig tree. After all it was not the season for figs, and He seemingly deals harshly with the tree. This would seem on the surface like an abuse of prophetic power.

Of course, my rationale was errant. Our Lord would never act impetuously and certainly would not abuse His power by inappropriate means. So what is the meaning of the cursing of the fig tree? Why did the Lord act in such a way before the cross? Why was this story preserved for us today?

The fig tree is a picture of the saints, as God has called the saints to be instant in season and out. Events that occur before the traditional season are a sign and prepare the way for what is to come. In demonstrating the curse of the fig tree, Jesus was demonstrating that God will generally demand a forerunner to declare His ways at a time that is normally ahead of the rule. This is the task of the saint.

The current church will be forced to flow in the dynamics of warfare that is coming. Many will enter the flow whole-heartedly, but those who do not respond to the call will be destroyed. God called the fig tree, and it did not respond. God was not pleased with this lack of response and so the tree became withered and died.

God is calling His church TODAY. Is He calling you? Will you react in a lazy or unresponsive manner? Will you compare yourself to the other "trees" in your particular grove of existence? Will you offer the answer that it is not yet time?

God is calling His saints to be pursuers of the fullness of God, pursuers of a holy walk, pursuers of the glory of God, pursuers of an understanding and appreciation of His heart. God is calling His saints to obedience to Him. If you respond to the call, you will experience a fullness and blessing beyond anything you have ever known. God's saints will catch on fire for the Lord and catch those around them on fire. What a wonderful prospect!

The Call To A Saints Movement

Often we are required to set aside the mind-sets we have gained in the past in order to be able to grasp fresh things that the Lord is revealing. To truly understand the designation of "saint," we must put away our traditional concepts of saintly living. We must allow the Lord to breathe fresh life upon scriptures that we have read many times before.

THE CURRENT CHURCH

The Apostle Paul classified many in the church as weak, sickly, or sleeping.

> **1 Corinthians 11:30** For this cause many are weak and sickly among you, and many sleep.

The context of this verse provides us with a wonderful teaching regarding communion with Jesus. How often have we focused on this verse and interpreted the meaning as a warning regarding the possibility of partaking of communion while having sin in our life. The reality of the passage is that we need to continue to meet with the Lord Jesus for the purposes of loving Him and gaining perspective as to what He wants us to accomplish.

In that same light when Paul speaks of partaking of the body and blood of Christ "unworthily," he is addressing our shortsighted attitude as to who God is and what He offers in and for our life.

Whenever we label something as having "worth," we commit to it. When we view it as optional, or worth less than something else, we give priority to the greater.

Inactivity regarding the things of God's Spirit will yield the weak and sickly climate of which Paul speaks. A result will be an unhealthy body that will be unable to fend off the assault of this world. Continuing in the enthusiasm of the development of the plan of God will cause the believer to stay young and vibrant in the spirit. Caleb was eighty years old but possessed the vitality of his youth. Moses at one hundred and twenty years of age was still strong and active in the service of God. If we stop progressing forward, we will begin to decay.

> **Hebrews 6:1** Therefore leaving the principles of the doctrine of Christ, let us go on unto perfection; not laying again the foundation of repentance from dead works, and of faith toward God...

Principle things are those that have already been established in our life. We must build upon them as opposed to camping upon them. Doctrine is meant to serve as a foundation and not as a retirement center. Additionally, the saints that have passed from this world are desirous of our moving forward into new terrain. Sometimes we are led to believe that we must carry on in the same manner as a famous predecessor. In business, a six-word maxim is a prescription for failure: "What would my predecessor have done?"

In the book of Hebrews, we are told in Chapter 12 that we are surrounded by a cloud of witnesses, which includes the mighty host of heaven's populace. A part of that group of people includes faith's Hall of Fame listed in Hebrews 11. These patriarchs are not watching for the purpose of ensuring their name and modes of ministry. Rather, they watch to see us carry on in the work of the Father.

> **Hebrews 12:1** Wherefore seeing we also are compassed about with so great a cloud of witnesses, let us lay aside every weight, and the sin which doth so easily beset us, and let us run with patience the race that is set before us...

Weights are the accumulation of past success and accomplishment. Sin is missing the mark of God's present assignment for you. God looks at His church in this compelling hour and calls us to duty. Grasping this promise of opportunity is the key to moving forth into this hour of victory.

WEAKNESS IS AN OPPORTUNITY

A wonderful thing about our God, and a blessing for us, is that He loves to move in the midst of our weakness. While the church may be weak, God views that weakness as a place to demonstrate His strength.

> **1 Corinthians 1:25-27** Because the foolishness of God is wiser than men; and the weakness of God is stronger than men. 26 For ye see your calling, brethren, how that not many wise men after the flesh, not many mighty, not many noble, are called: 27 But God hath chosen the foolish things of the world to confound the wise; and God hath chosen the weak things of the world to confound the things which are mighty;

Weakness is not blight but a step toward power. God chooses the weak things in order to display His might. He wants to show His strength through a climate of dependency so He continually allows us to be in situations where we recognize our weakness. Once we are able to face our weakness without shame before men and God, our weakness becomes an opportunity for God to demonstrate His power.

A SLEEPING CHURCH

When Paul said in 1 Corinthians 11:30 that many sleep, he was not simply utilizing the verb as a euphemism for death in the natural. The Greek word ***koimesis*** is used also to depict those who slumber so soundly that they might as well be dead. This same word is used in the scriptures as a point of reference for three other characteristics that may be helpful in defining a slumbering church. The church can be described as sleeping in ignorance, in hopelessness, or in denial.

- **Sleeping In Ignorance**

    Acts 12:6-7 And when Herod would have brought him forth, the same night Peter was sleeping between two soldiers, bound with two chains: and the keepers before the door kept the prison. 7 And, behold, the angel of the Lord came upon him, and a light shined in the prison: and he smote Peter on the side, and raised him up, saying, Arise up quickly. And his chains fell off from his hands.

Peter was sleeping soundly between two guards in prison. He was so out of touch with reality that the angel of deliverance God sent had to go to great lengths to get his attention. Like Peter, the church sleeps in chains enduring the bondage of the enemy. This ignorance yields blissful repose, but repose nonetheless. It also yields dullness to the presence of God's deliverance even when it is sent specifically for them.

> **Mark 13:35-37** Watch ye therefore: for ye know not when the master of the house cometh, at even, or at midnight, or at the cockcrowing, or in the morning: 36 Lest coming suddenly he find

you sleeping. 37 And what I say unto you I say unto all, Watch.

Apparently when the Lord returns, He will find many who are asleep. He lists four differing timeframes that entice people to sleepiness. The evening would speak of our feeling that the workday has concluded, so we need not do any further work. Midnight is a time that is scripturally famous for sudden visitations of the Lord but is often missed because people consider that hour as their time to rightfully be asleep. How often in our lives have we resented the crowing of the cock or the sounding of the alarm clock? Sleeping well into the morning will generally represent the sluggard.

Neither weariness, personal rights, lack of industriousness, or laziness are excuses that will pre-empt us from the necessity of being ready for the Lord's return. God's remedy is simply "Watch."

- **Sleeping In Hopelessness**

    Luke 22:45 And when he rose up from prayer, and was come to his disciples, he found them sleeping for sorrow.

In the Garden of Gethsemane the Lord Jesus found the three disciples sleeping for sorrow. He lamented that they needed to watch and pray, but instead they could not tarry in prayer even for one hour. To be asleep for the sake of sorrow is a classic case of hopeless despair. It readily implies a failure to see the bigger picture of what God is doing. The Spirit of the Lord is willing, but a fixation on the fleshly vantage point will render us inoperative.

The Lord stands with us at another crucial point in the timetable, and because of fear or for some other human deferment, we are reluctant to join Him in His hour of need. We have covenanted in an attempt to keep ourselves from risk. Like the ostrich in the sand, we hide our heads in a farcical attempt to escape the time of challenge.

> **1 Thessalonians 5:6-7** Therefore let us not sleep, as do others; but let us watch and be sober. 7 For they that sleep sleep in the night; and they that be drunken are drunken in the night.

Much of the church will be found sleeping in the end time. Those who are sober will watch and pray.

- **Sleeping In Denial**

Sadly, many within the church will deny the power of the resurrection. Immediately following the resurrection of Jesus, the enemy was already at work to begin this process of denial. The Jewish authorities instructed the guards, who watched over the

Tomb of Resurrection, to say that Jesus' disciples had come and stolen away His dead body while the guards were sleeping.

> **Matthew 28:13** Saying, Say ye, His disciples came by night, and stole him away while we slept.

Many within the church will deny that God is doing anything special in this day of great opportunity. For many varied reasons they choose not to participate in the Lord's plan while using their mouths to discredit the validity of His power. The enemy is always looking for a discrediting mouthpiece. He usually finds his most potent weapon within the very ranks of the church. Talebearers yield strife; and where strife is, every evil work can find a niche.

When Jesus dealt with the death of Jairus' daughter, He told the hired disbelievers that the girl was only asleep. Like these mourners, there are many such vessels within the modern church who are equally adept at any type of negative expression.

> **Luke 8:52-53** And all wept, and bewailed her: but he said, Weep not; she is not dead, but sleepeth. 53 And they laughed him to scorn, knowing that she was dead.

This is truly a picture of the modern church world: ridiculing the representative of Christ and verbally discrediting the possibility of a miracle in the now. The power of our Lord and our belief in Him turns doubt and dark reality into life and victory.

TIME TO WAKE UP

So whether it is because of denial, hopelessness, or just plain ignorance, much of the church is slumbering while the call of the Lord comes forth.

> **Joel 3:9-11** Proclaim ye this among the Gentiles; Prepare war, wake up the mighty men, let all the men of war draw near; let them come up: 10 Beat your plowshares into swords, and your pruninghooks into spears: let the weak say, I am strong. 11 Assemble yourselves, and come, all ye heathen, and gather yourselves together round about: thither cause thy mighty ones to come down, O LORD.

God is declaring that the mighty men must wake up! He is instructing them to prepare their implements of war and to be made strong in Him. He is sending His mighty men from the heavens to join with those who have roused themselves from slumber. The church has the ability to follow hard after God. It is not that she cannot heed the call, but rather that she *will not* heed the call. Weariness is not an accepted rationale, for rest and refreshing are readily available to those who will hear the Lord.

> **Isaiah 28:12** To whom he said, This is the rest wherewith ye may cause the weary to rest; and this is the refreshing: yet they would not hear.

Many in the church are very comfortable in their spiritual inactivity; and if they are even able to hear the call, they simply turn over and continue in their slumber. Those in the church who are out of the will of God will be likely targets for the enemy. Even the Apostle Paul prophesied that the great move of the last days would not come without the prerequisite of a falling away.

> **2 Thessalonians 2:3** Let no man deceive you by any means: for that day shall not come, except there come a falling away first, and that man of sin be revealed, the son of perdition;

A Sobering Epithet

God is calling the mighty men, His saints, in this hour. To those who will heed the call to battle, the greatest hour lies ahead; but those who fail to heed the call are given a stirring and sobering word of warning.

> **Judges 5:23** Curse ye Meroz, said the angel of the LORD, curse ye bitterly the inhabitants thereof; because they came not to the help of the LORD, to the help of the LORD against the mighty.

To those mighty ones who will come to the aid of the cause of the Lord, there will be a magnificent victory. Those who do not, like the men of Meroz, will be cursed. The curse will be manifold in depiction and will be commensurate with the tragedies that are outlined in the eschatological passages of the Word of God. God help us to heed the saintly call.

Establishing The Kingdom

4

God is calling the saints for the purpose of transacting His business on this planet. As soon as there is a response to the call, God begins a training process designed to equip the saint for kingdom conquest and rule. In the Book of Ephesians, we are told that the saint should be experiencing training concerning the dimensions of the Kingdom of God.

> **Ephesians 3:14-19** For this cause I bow my knees unto the Father of our Lord Jesus Christ, 15 Of whom the whole family in heaven and earth is named, 16 That he would grant you, according to the riches of his glory, to be strengthened with might by his Spirit in the inner man; 17 That Christ may dwell in your hearts by faith; that ye, being rooted and grounded in love, 18 May be able to **comprehend** with all saints what is the breadth, and length, and depth, and height; 19 And to know the love of Christ, which passeth knowledge, that ye might be filled with all the fulness of God.

Within this passage we ascertain the exploratory and apostolic dimension of the saints. God will allow the saints to comprehend the secret expanses of His vast dominion. These do not solely consist of places and realms but contain the very schematics of the truths of the Kingdom of God. When we read about breadth, length, depth and height, we envision architectural significance. Like a caring Father, our God wants His children to know the fullness of what belongs to them. He desires for them to understand these realities in great detail.

The word for **comprehend** in Verse 18 is the Greek word ***katalambano*** which means to understand and to control something by virtue of that understanding. ***Katalambano*** is utilized by John in the first chapter of his Gospel to tell of the absolute dominance of God's light whenever it is shined into darkness.

> **John 1:5** And the light shineth in darkness; and the darkness **comprehended** it not.

It is also utilized by Paul in order to describe how he was overtaken and apprehended by the knowledge and love of Christ Jesus.

> **Philippians 3:12** Not as though I had already attained, either were already perfect: but I follow after, if that I may **apprehend** that for which also I am **apprehended** of Christ Jesus.

When we view this powerful word in reference to the saints, it illuminates that they will move mightily in a domineering understanding of the full dimensions of the Kingdom of God. This understanding when properly applied will not be successfully withstood and can overcome any opposition.

Knowledge is power and is essential in establishing the works of God in the world that He created. Perhaps the most prolific tool against ignorance and deception is the weapon of information and truth. The enemy hates revealed knowledge. He will fight against reception and appropriation of the mysteries of the Lord.

Perhaps the most compelling phraseology found in these verses are the words "apprehend" and "apprehended." Comprehending the things of the Kingdom will do you little good unless you are apprehended by God and in pursuit of apprehending more and more of Him. Without a passionate devotional exchange between you and the Heavenly Father, no amount of insight will suffice. There will simply be no meaning. Knowledge will pass away, but the love exchanged between you and your Creator will last eternally.

One further thought is also significant to this discussion. If you are not involved in a love relationship with God, you will not possess the strength and fortitude to withstand the enemy opposition that will come against the secrets of the Kingdom. This is why love is said to be the greatest of all spiritual gifts.

FOUR DIRECTIONAL PURSUITS OF THE SAINTS

In Romans 8 Paul associates this spatial dimension with creatures that withstand the process of development and assignment.

> **Romans 8:38-39** For I am persuaded, that neither death, nor life, nor angels, nor principalities, nor powers, nor things present, nor things to come, 39 Nor height, nor depth, nor any other creature, shall be able to separate us from the love of God, which is in Christ Jesus our Lord.

When he says "nor any other creature," the Apostle Paul reveals an added dimension to the discussion of dimensional reality. It is my opinion that these "creatures" are the enemies that crouch at the gates of entry into the deeper things of God. God references this in His discussion with Cain in the Book of Genesis.

> **Genesis 4:7** If thou doest well, shalt thou not be accepted? and if thou doest not well, sin lieth at the door. And unto thee shall be his desire, and thou shalt rule over him.

These opposing entities are obviously different than the other mentioned influences within this passage, all of which are readily known within the spirit realm. Undoubtedly, there are specific opponents that position themselves at the very entry into the deeper things of God. For Cain, they struck at his insecurity and subsequent disobedience to the command of God. Undoubtedly, these foes will attack us in the same manner.

Our Father is so vast, and He desires to bring us into His presence in ways that are beyond our ability to comprehend with the mind. The enemy does not want this commune to occur. He knows that with every insight of relationship, the believer becomes stronger and more devoted in the pursuit of the Father's business.

Vertical opposition is that which will seek to prohibit you from advancing into the higher things of the Kingdom of God. These opponents are concerned because as you move higher into the places of God's choosing, this will mean certain demotion and doom for them. So, they will fight against you with all that is within them.

Depth speaks of foundational footing. How well are you grounded for your development? How deep are your roots of supply and strength? This dimension has to do with that which takes place within our earthly setting. Quite literally, we are establishing the Kingdom of Heaven within the depths of the earth.

Our depth in the love of God is of utmost importance. As we fall deeper in love with the Almighty, our relationship is developed to the degree that He can trust us with greater responsibility. Depth represents foundation. Foundational integrity is essential for any building of substance. The building of our faith will soar in accordance with the deepness of our foundation of love and trust in the Heavenly Father. Without a deep relationship, there can be no trust. Without trust there can be no revelation of partnership and subsequently no development and operation.

Of all of the directional dimensions, depth of love and relationship with God is foundationally most important. No wonder the enemy attacks it most voraciously.

In summation, we must forge our way through the heavens as we gain authorities in God. From our heavenly seats, we will rule and reign with God. As a result of this placement, we will establish God's righteousness upon the earth. These appointments will necessitate the clearing away of opposition that has wrongfully inhabited the place of God's intended rule.

EARNEST EXPECTATIONS

God created the earth for a specific intention, and He created mankind in order to implement that divine design. When Adam and Eve were deceived, the world was thrown into a cycle that was not God's original desire. The saints are designated to partner with

God in taking back the earth. Creation knows this and longs for the culmination of God's ordained intention.

> **Romans 8:19** For the earnest expectation of the creature waiteth for the manifestation of the sons of God.

In so many ways, what God initially intended for this planet was interrupted by the rebellion of Lucifer. Adam was to have been the partner of God in restoring the created intent of the footstool of the Lord's glory; but when he disobeyed God, the plan was put on hold once more. Quite literally, the Kingdom of God is a portrayal of what God intends for this planet, and the blueprint is awaiting our discovery and implementation. Creation is waits with an earnest expectation for the saints to look into the original plans of God, into the things that He intended from the beginning, and to partner with Him in the incredible process of re-establishing His Kingdom.

MANIFESTATION

God said in Amos 3:7 that he would not do anything until he first revealed it to his friends, the prophets. There is something within the heart of God that loves intrigue and the subsequent revelation of mystery. While these mysteries will ultimately be known by the entire world, they are first shown to those that are classified as His friends.

In this eighth chapter of Romans, we are told that creation waits for a revelation of the sons of God. This is a reference to the actual unveiling of these sons, but also the mystery that is revealed to them. The word for **mystery** in this passage is *apokalupsis,* a colorful word that means to take the lid off of a container and look within.

The Word of God tells us that the process of gleaning these types of *apokalupsis* revelations is one that involves groaning and birthing. There are many such revelations within the heart of God, and He looks for intercessors that will conceive the process of revelation and travail it through until birth. Consider this process as it is displayed throughout creation.

> **Romans 8:22-23** For we know that the whole creation groaneth and travaileth in pain together until now. 23 And not only they, but ourselves also, which have the firstfruits of the Spirit, even we ourselves groan within ourselves, waiting for the adoption, to wit, the redemption of our body.

The sons of God are coming, and they are receiving "firstfruits of the spirit." This can only be a reference to the figs that ripen before the general harvest, the meat that provides for the mighty move of God that is to come.

Apokalupsis is used to characterize much of what is going to happen from this time forward. The Revelation of St. John is literally the *apokalupsis* of St. John. John was a lover of Jesus and also a passionate follower of the Heavenly Father. Something hidden was revealed to him concerning what was to come. We are living in those days, and creation is awaiting our grasp of what God will say to his sons.

> **Romans 16:25** Now to him that is of power to stablish you according to my gospel, and the preaching of Jesus Christ, according to the revelation of the **mystery**, which was kept secret since the world began,

The earth was created to be a showcase of the glory of the Lord, and it yearns for the showing forth of the sons of God. The earth longs for the Holy Ghost to show us the places where the enemy has entrenchments and footholds. It longs to be free from the enslavement of the enemy and is groaning for the liberating move of God.

This is why Jesus said that there would be earthquakes, signs in the heavens above and in the earth beneath. The revelation of the mysteries of God to the saints and the subsequent appropriation and application of these mysteries is being met with excitement by creation. We will go head to head with strongholds that the enemy has held for much too long a time. Ultimately, the righteous purpose of God will be revealed in judgment upon the earth. This will dictate corrective measures against many things that have become commonplace upon the earth, but that are far from the original intent of God.

> **Romans 2:5** But after thy hardness and impenitent heart treasurest up unto thyself wrath against the day of wrath and **revelation** of the righteous judgment of God;

Apokalupsis is the masterplan of God for His creation. The manner in which these powerful truths are made known is through an orderly process of discovery that transpires between God and His servants.

The Saints

Building Up The Saints

God has been preserving information about the saints for an end-time revelation. The time of Revelation is upon us. At the conclusion of the Book of Daniel, the angel of the Lord tells him that the scroll of revelation would be sealed until the time of the end, and this scroll is currently being unveiled.

END-TIME REVELATION

> **Daniel 8:17** So he came near where I stood: and when he came, I was afraid, and fell upon my face: but he said unto me, Understand, O son of man: for at the time of the end shall be the vision.
>
> **Daniel 12:4** But thou, O Daniel, shut up the words, and seal the book, even to the time of the end: many shall run to and fro, and knowledge shall be increased.
>
> **Daniel 12:8, 9** And I heard, but I understood not: then said I, O my Lord, what shall be the end of these things? 9 And he said, Go thy way, Daniel: for the words are closed up and sealed till the time of the end.

We are now living in the days of God's end-time revelation. To cooperate with God in this hour, we must press into Him in intercession and accountability as did Daniel. In reading through the Book of Daniel, we find a man of great intelligence and ability who laid his talents at the feet of God. He prayed and submitted his life toward the call of God. The price of partnering with God has not diminished since the days of Daniel. For those who participate in the unfolding of these insights, a Daniel-like devotion will be necessary.

RHEMA

Whenever God wants to reveal a specific and pertinent word for a moment in time, He does so through a *rhema* word. In the New Testament *rhema* words are exceptionally important for the growth and safety of the believer. For instance, in Ephesians 6 *rhema* is essential for victory in warfare.

> **Ephesians 6:17**... and the sword of the Spirit, which is the **word** of God:

The Greek noun for **word** in this verse is *rhema*. God reveals these intimate and strategic revelations to those who are searching for Him. To any who are on the frontier of service to God, *rhema* words will mean the difference between victory, defeat, or stagnation. The *rhema* of God will flow through commune with Him. Jesus said that this type of Godly expression comes directly from the mouth of the Father and is essential for life.

> **Matthew 4:4** But he answered and said, It is written, Man shall not live by bread alone, but by every **word** that proceedeth out of the mouth of God.

Sometimes this will be depicted by virtue of a prophetic insight, dream, or vision. Often God will illumine a passage of scripture, and the *logos* becomes a *rhema* for the hour. The *rhema* word will always be in harmony with the written Word of God.

RESISTANCE TO *RHEMA*

A *rhema* anointing is generally necessary for acquisition and belief. Jesus encountered a lack of such anointing in this account found in the Gospel of Luke.

> **Luke 9:45-46** But they understood not this saying, and it was hid from them, that they perceived it not: and they feared to ask him of that saying. 46 Then there arose a reasoning among them, which of them should be greatest.

The disciples did not understand his *rhema* for it had not been revealed to them personally. They could not grasp the meaning, and the Bible says that they were inclined to avoid the revelation. Their reaction led into a prideful discussion.

The church world today is in need of *rhema* from the Father; but when *rhema* comes, we are inclined to resist the revelation perceiving it as being "too deep," impractical, or unscriptural. Ultimately, this is a result of pride and an unwillingness to let God change us. We must be quick to hear and slow to speak. Do not resist new revelation upon initial presentation, let it find its place. We need fresh *rhema*.

OPPOSITION FROM ENEMY *RHEMA*

> **Matthew 5:11** Blessed are ye, when men shall revile you, and persecute you, and shall say all manner of *evil* against you falsely, for my sake.

In this well-known passage the word for **evil** is *rhema*. The enemy knows the power of *rhema* to the degree that he will regularly use the Word of God, and the principles of the Word, to his advantage. Often this enemy *rhema* will come against God's people. Sometimes this will take the form of directed curses from the enemy camp, and other times it can innocently result from the gossip circles of ignorant critics. Rest assured that the enemy will use *rhema* in the battle against the saints. When we speak of the ministers of unrighteousness in Chapter 12, we will deal with this concept in greater detail.

AGNOSTICOSTALS

It has been said that the opposite of love is not hate but indifference. If there is a more disastrous thing than resistance, it is perhaps indifference. Jesus characterized this as lukewarmness, and it should have no place in the life of the believer. Many Christians are lukewarm when it comes to new revelation or any fresh insight concerning the things of the Spirit. Paul warns the Corinthian church against such lack of feeling.

> **1 Corinthians 12:1** Now concerning spiritual gifts, brethren, I would not have you ***ignorant***.

In this passage the Greek term for **ignorant** is *agnoeo* meaning to be disinclined or to ignore. Pentecostals who are this way should be called agnosticostals. They are Spirit baptized but do not want to know if there is anything further for them in God beyond their current experience.

Whenever a pioneering reality and responsibility of the church is discussed, if it does not appear to be enticing or easy, most believers are reluctant to champion the message. Like the reception of *rhema,* there is an opposition to the new. "If God is moving in a way that is different than what I have known, I do not really want to know about it!" Pride? Yes. Laziness? Perhaps. An attitude filled with indifference is just the same.

Agnoeo can be dangerous for other reasons. For one, indifference can render you vulnerable to Satan.

> **2 Corinthians 2:11** Lest Satan should get an advantage of us: for we are not ***ignorant*** of his devices.

Indifference of this sort will provide the enemy with an advantage over you. A lack of current revelation will render you unequipped in the face of the enemy and will deprive you of the equipping that the rest of the saints have received from God. Much of the general church is languishing in this vulnerable state of existence. To deny fresh revelation of the movements of our God is to deny our ongoing purpose and place in Him.

In this passage we are not to be indifferent to the devices of the enemy. **Devices** is the Greek word *noema*, or the root word in *agnoeo*. *Noema* is a wonderfully selected word meaning purpose. The enemy has a purpose, too, and that is to stop you from realizing God's purpose for your life.

In the Book of 2 Corinthians we are told of several other enemies of the purpose of God in the life of the believer. These enemies will attack your growth as well as your effectiveness. Let us look at these enemies of saintly purpose.

PRINCIPALITY

The god of this world will battle the non-believer as well as the carnal Christian in order to render them blinded to what God has in store for them. If they do not see the purpose of God, they will not step into freedom.

> **2 Corinthians 4:4** In whom the god of this world hath blinded the **minds** of them which believe not, lest the light of the glorious gospel of Christ, who is the image of God, should shine unto them.

The enemy will also move subtly against all of the church to attempt to confuse the purpose of God in the thinking of believers. Just as Eve was beguiled to misconstrue what God was saying, so our purpose is under attack by the same devious agent of confusion.

> **2 Corinthians 11:3** But I fear, lest by any means, as the serpent beguiled Eve through his subtilty, so your **minds** should be corrupted from the simplicity that is in Christ.

Following Christ is a complicated, yet simple reality. The intricacies of the Father's plan are vast, but step by step He makes them simple enough for us to understand. The enemy cannot stop God's purpose, but he will attempt to confuse the junctures of revelation and obedience.

RELIGIOUS MINDSET

Noema appears again in discussion concerning Moses. Here the revelation of fresh purpose to the people of Israel is not readily received. Whether the blinding cited within this passage is of the enemy or religiosity, it is blinding nonetheless.

> **2 Corinthians 3:14** But their **minds** were blinded: for until this day remaineth the same vail untaken away in the reading of the old testament; which vail is done away in Christ.

Although this passage refers to the hindering influences that keep the Jewish people from seeing the reality of Christ, it is an indicator of any type of religious yoke. The veil is done away in Christ, which simply means that clarity comes as we commit ourselves to move in the anointing of the Holy Spirit in order to accomplish the Father's plan.

REMEDY

Whenever we are presented with a new truth from the Lord, we must always submit it to our Lord Jesus Christ. Jesus became the Christ as He submitted Himself continually to the empowering of the Holy Spirit to accomplish the Father's bidding. Paul says that we must always align our *noema*, or any *noema*, to the obedience of Christ. This will ensure that we are continually committed to the purposes of God.

> **2 Corinthians 10:5** Casting down imaginations, and every high thing that exalteth itself against the knowledge of God, and bringing into captivity every **thought** to the obedience of Christ;

Our thinking must always be in alignment with the *noema* of God, as the natural mind will tend to want its own way. Paul's epistle to the Philippians speaks candidly of this truth.

> **Philippians 4:7-8** And the peace of God, which passeth all understanding, shall keep your hearts and **minds** through Christ Jesus. 8 Finally, brethren, whatsoever things are true, whatsoever things are honest, whatsoever things are just, whatsoever things are pure, whatsoever things are lovely, whatsoever things are of good report; if there be any virtue, and if there be any praise, think on these things.

The point is that we must be ready to receive information from the sources of God's choosing. We must also recognize that the enemy and our carnal mind will jointly attack our reception of this *noema*. It is essential that we remain willing to receive such insight.

MYSTERIES

Within the pages of the last chapter, an understanding of *apokalupsis* was detailed. The manner in which *apokalupsis* is made known is through progressive unveiling of the heart of God. These layers are shown in the New Testament in the person of the Greek word *musterion*, a word that is largely translated as mystery, but it is much different than *apokalusis*.

If *apokalupsis* is the gift, *musterion* is the layered casing that must be systematically unwrapped. If *apokalupsis* is the mystery novel, *musterion* is the unfolding plot. It would be fair to classify *apokalupsis* with the *chronos* purpose of God and *musterion* with the progressive *kairos* unveilings of His timetable.

Of many verses, this association of revelation is most clearly seen in Romans 16.

> **Romans 16:25** Now to him that is of power to stablish you according to my gospel, and the preaching of Jesus Christ, according to the revelation (**apokalupsis**) of the **mystery (musterion)**, which was kept secret since the world began,

Musterion has been hid in God from the beginning of all things alongside *apokalupsis*. This progressive understanding of *musterion* is classified as a fellowship in the Book of Ephesians.

> **Ephesians 3:9** And to make all men see what is the fellowship of the **mystery**, which from the beginning of the world hath been hid in God, who created all things by Jesus Christ.

Musterion is a powerful topic in the New Testament. Let us examine some examples of how God will reveal His *apokalupsis* through *musterion*.

It is clear that God is not intent upon making His mysteries clear to just everyone. Jesus cloaked the understanding of *musterion* in parables.

> **Luke 8:10** And he said, Unto you it is given to know the **mysteries** of the kingdom of God: but to others in parables; that seeing they might not see, and hearing they might not understand.

He still makes these progressive understandings known in ways that are seemingly obtuse. To those that will pursue them, there is a measure of the glory of the Lord that will be provided to the recipient.

> **1 Corinthians 2:7** But we speak the wisdom of God in a **mystery**, even the hidden wisdom, which God ordained before the world unto our glory:

These longstanding mysteries are reserved for the saints.

> **Colossians 1:26** Even the **mystery** which hath been hid from ages and from generations, but now is made manifest to his saints:

To the saints, these mysteries are precious. When they are revealed, the saint must treat them very carefully. The word classifies this responsibility as stewardship.

> **1 Corinthians 4:1** Let a man so account of us, as of the ministers of Christ, and stewards of the **mysteries** of God.

You will never participate in the process of a saintly walk and the dimension of revelation until you commune regularly with the Heavenly Father. Enoch walked with God. We must learn to walk with Him as well. This is what Adam and Eve were created to do. It is apparent that God is intent upon finding people that will commune with Him and allow His heart to be revealed to them. The heart of God is so vast and His ways so compelling that there is a place for all who desire intimate relationship. This type of relationship will afford the individual the incredible opportunity of knowing what God is going to do before He actually does it.

Every person to whom God chooses to reveal His mysteries has a desire to know what God is saying now. For them there is no other option. Why would we want another option? Commune with the Father is the apex of our capacity. Nothing else compares. This revealed manifestation will not only change you, but it will change the world.

The truth is something different than the accumulation of revealed knowledge that we doctrinally possess. The truth will encompass the salient revelation of the gospel of Jesus Christ as a principle foundation. We build upon a rock, and loving devotion to Him is our foundation.

These mysteries will be revealed in various ways.

- **Angelic Sources**

Insights will come directly from the Lord through His angels and their ministry to us. Since much of the activity of the saint will be in accordance with angelic interaction, it is vital that we see an extremely important truth. Daniel was continually in contact with the angelic. There are some that would decry the angelic as a source of information, but God continually uses them to bring messages. The word angel means messenger. In Daniel 8, God Himself is speaking to Daniel, then He assigns Gabriel the task of continued communicative input into Daniel's life.

> **Daniel 8:16** And I heard a man's voice between the banks of Ulai, which called, and said, Gabriel, make this man to understand the vision.

> **Daniel 9:22** And he informed me, and talked with me, and said, O Daniel, I am now come forth to give thee skill and understanding.

Gabriel is told by the Father to give understanding of a vision to Daniel, so Gabriel grants skill and understanding to Daniel. The Father was obviously present to communicate as He talked with Gabriel, yet He appointed an angel to interact with Daniel.

What skill and understanding were given? Undoubtedly, God granted him the skill to find what had not been seen by natural means. Skill was granted for the procuring of new truths, and understanding as to what they meant and how they should be applied.

- **Patriarchal Sources**

Insights will also come from other sources already within the heavenlies. Daniel 8 details an incident in which Daniel received information from a heavenly saint:

> **Daniel 8:13** Then I heard one saint speaking, and another saint said unto that certain saint which spake, How long shall be the vision concerning the daily sacrifice, and the transgression of desolation, to give both the sanctuary and the host to be trodden under foot?

John spoke with a prophet and fellow servant in heaven:

> **Revelation 22:8-9** And I John saw these things, and heard them. And when I had heard and seen, I fell down to worship before the feet of the angel which shewed me these things. 9 Then saith he unto me, See thou do it not: for I am thy fellowservant, and of thy brethren the prophets, and of them which keep the sayings of this book: worship God.

Jesus conferred with Moses and Elijah on the Mount of Transfiguration while Peter, James and John were present:

> **Mark 9:4** And there appeared unto *them* Elias with Moses: and they were talking with Jesus

- **Enemy Counterfeit**

Just as the Word reveals that these sources are available to His saints, the enemy has utilized this available pathway of insight through the horror of necromancy. King Saul consulted the witch of Endor to "conjure up" the patriarch Samuel.

> **1 Samuel 28:15** And Samuel said to Saul, Why hast thou disquieted me, to bring me up? And Saul answered, I am sore distressed; for the Philistines make war against me, and God is departed from me, and answereth me no more, neither by prophets, nor by dreams: therefore I have called thee, that thou mayest make known unto me what I shall do.

In no way do I mean to imply that we consult with patriarchs of our choosing at a time of our own fancy. Interaction or consultations with patriarchs will be divine appointments. Either the Word of God is true or it is not. When we come to our Mount Zion, we do so with, among others, a great cloud of witnesses. These are universally regarded as being representatives of the "Hall of Faith."

> **Hebrews 12:22-23** But ye are come unto mount Sion, and unto the city of the living God, the heavenly Jerusalem, and to an innumerable company of angels, 23 To the general assembly and church of the firstborn, which are written in

heaven, and to God the Judge of all, and to the spirits of just men made perfect...

As stated earlier, we come to our Mount Zion in the presence of the general assembly, the spirits of just men made perfect that comprise the agents of righteousness, and the church of the firstborn, which are the pioneers of apostolic invention.

It is imperative that we remain open to receiving information from God in ways that are additional to the norm. The Holy Ghost will guide us into all truth and show us things to come. Undoubtedly these measures will include the ways that have been recorded in the Book that He authored – the written Word of God.

THE END OF MYSTERY

The concept of *musterion* is continuing in powerful ways. The Bible tells us that we are rapidly approaching a time when this process of revelation will have reached its conclusion.

> **Revelation 10:7** But in the days of the voice of the seventh angel, when he shall begin to sound, the **mystery** of God should be finished, as he hath declared to his servants the prophets.

There is a well-known parable about the time of the end that speaks of the church, particularly focusing upon the second coming of the Lord. It is the passage involving the ten virgins.

Matthew 25:1-3 Then shall the kingdom of heaven be likened unto ten virgins, which took their lamps, and went forth to meet the bridegroom. 2 And five of them were wise, and five were **foolish**. 3 They that were **foolish** took their lamps, and took no oil with them:

The word for **foolish** is *moros*, and it is a derivative of *musterion*. Within this parable are many concepts, but most prominent for this discussion is the idea of mystery that leads to the coming of our Lord. Those within the church that seek His *musterion* will be prepared for His coming. Those foolish virgins that rely upon someone else to gain understanding will miss Him.

Set aside your concepts of eternal security for a moment and look at the imperative nature of this parable. Are we really desirous of being so close to God that we continually partner with Him in His program of revelation?

These virgins held lamps, which speak of knowing something that is immediately ahead. According to the Book of Revelation, the lamp is a symbol of the winds of the Spirit of God. Do we know Him well enough to be in continual harmony with His ways?

There are five wise virgins, and this could easily represent the five-fold ministry that God is mightily emphasizing in this hour. Are we fully accepting this commission from our Lord?

An Undeniable Call

> **Jude 1** Beloved, when I gave all diligence to write unto you of the common salvation, it was needful for me to write unto you, and exhort you that ye should earnestly contend for the faith which was once delivered unto the saints.

"Once delivered" means that there is a unique calling within the life of each person, and that calling will not waver within the span of a lifetime. While the calling that is submitted to God will develop and mature, God will not repent or change His mind concerning the purpose that He desires for an individual. We cannot exchange our calling with someone else. We cannot choose for ourselves what God has purposed for our spiritual service. Quite the contrary! Our calling must be earnestly pursued. It will be opposed; therefore, we must contend for it. This is not an easy undertaking. The contribution of each saint is invaluable in nature and scope. Like the construction of a great building or the fulfilling of a multi-faceted project, the part played by each willing believer is paramount for success of the project.

> **Ephesians 2:21** In whom all the building fitly framed together groweth unto an holy temple in the Lord:

A Graceful Conversion

The Christian life is a progression. God continually desires to change us from what we currently are into what He desires. You can choose to do nothing on the hope of being able to squeak into heaven someday; but change is not optional to those who want to progress into the deeper and higher things of God.

> **2 Corinthians 3:18** But we all, with open face beholding as in a glass the glory of the Lord, are changed into the same image from glory to glory, even as by the Spirit of the Lord.

Change is an odd thing. We say that we want it, until it comes time to change. Then we only want to change what we deem necessary. This process is especially hard on those who are happy with where they are in the Lord. Perhaps they are in a position of fulfillment. Perhaps people look up to them. Wealthy landholders do not make good pioneers. What is the motivation for moving forward? They already think they "have it made." Jesus said that those who are rich in this world would have a hard time entering into the Kingdom.

> **Mark 10:24-26** And the disciples were astonished at his words. But Jesus answereth again, and saith unto them, Children, how hard is it for them that trust in riches to enter into the kingdom of God! 25 It is easier for a camel to go through the eye of a needle, than for a rich man to enter into the kingdom of God. 26 And they were astonished out of measure...

By virtue of their astonishment, the disciples mirrored the mindset of most of the world. We are programmed to the ideal of becoming more and more affluent. The Lord tells us that if we are going to continually enjoy access into His Kingdom, we have to be willing to give up everything that we currently possess. If we love the things that we possess, they possess us. Giving all that we have is the ticket into the Kingdom of Heaven.

Entering into the Kingdom is a terminology that is widely regarded to mean becoming born again. However, in studying the Word, we have to enter into the Kingdom with each phase of development in God. This does not mean that we must be "born again" at every phase of developmental change. Yet, change we must, and change we will if we desire to flow in the glory of the present truths of the Lord. Jesus told His disciples that they needed to be converted as little children.

> **Matthew 18:3** And said, Verily I say unto you, Except ye be converted, and become as little children, ye shall not enter into the kingdom of heaven.

He was not speaking these words to a group of unrepentant vagabonds. Rather, He spoke them to His current disciples. Entering the Kingdom meant being something other than born again or the teaching would not make sense.

The root meaning of conversion involves the idea of becoming something new and different. In order to enter into the new things that God is doing, we must be willing to allow God to change us. Jesus spoke about this conversion reality when he was speaking to Peter:

> **Luke 22:32** But I have prayed for thee, that thy faith fail not: and when thou art converted, strengthen thy brethren.

Peter was already born again, but Jesus said that a change was necessary in Peter's life in order for him to be able to minister in a more effective manner. He implies that this conversion will also be necessary for the other disciples. The Apostle Paul spoke of having the same need within his life.

> **Philippians 3:12** Not as though I had already attained, either were already perfect: but I follow after, if that I may apprehend that for which also I am apprehended of Christ Jesus.

If Paul and Peter needed this ministry, we must also be freshly converted throughout our Christian walk. Grace is required for this transaction to occur.

SAVED BY GRACE

Grace is a curious dimension within the workings of our God. People only think of grace as being "Amazing," rarely considing what it means beyond the born-again experience. In the Book of Ephesians we find how grace starts with us in the way of life and continues to advance and promote us through every stage of development.

> **Ephesians 2:5-8** Even when we were dead in sins, hath quickened us together with Christ, (by grace ye are saved;) 6 And hath raised us up together, and made us sit together in heavenly places in Christ Jesus: 7 That in the ages to come he might shew the exceeding riches of his grace in his kindness toward us through Christ Jesus. 8 For by grace are ye saved through faith; and that not of yourselves: it is the gift of God:

The traditional definition of grace is God's unmerited favor. Grace literally lifts us from where we are and carries us to a higher place in Him. Whenever God wants to promote or to bring us into a more advanced realm in Him, He utilizes grace. Grace does not cease with the salvation prayer. The verses just cited state that the process of grace will continue in us throughout the ages to come.

Certainly God desires for us to continue to flow within the power of grace in every facet of our existence on this earth.

> **2 Peter 3:18** But grow in grace, and in the knowledge of our Lord and Saviour Jesus Christ. To him be glory both now and for ever. Amen.

THE THRONE OF GRACE

The Word of God says that God sits on a throne that is made of grace.

> **Hebrews 4:16** Let us therefore come boldly unto the throne of grace, that we may obtain mercy, and find grace to help in time of need.

Those who have seen the throne of God will probably say that it is constructed of a material that is unlike any known to human builders. This is literally grace. Sometimes the Lord has allowed me to perceive a touch of grace upon individuals. This generally indicates that God is trying to promote them into the next phase of development.

While God is always interested in meeting our needs, our time of need is not necessarily referring to our temporal challenges. Rather, this speaks of coming before the Throne of Grace for the sake of promotion. The time of need comes when we recognize that we are being called to a fresh positioning of son-ship, and that we cannot make it on our own. God allows us to find His mercy as we boldly pursue our place in Him.

Mercy is the love of God that always abides and grants the possibility of provision, but grace must be found and accepted. This is a foreign concept to most. Grace being searched for, what does that mean? Anything that is worth something in the Lord must be found in Him. God has quite a reputation in the scriptures for seeing how much you really want Him. We must find grace; and when we do, it holds the miracle power of God for favor and victory.

DISPENSATIONS OF GRACE

Since grace is a developmental element, rarely does God just grant a ready-made fulfillment of grace. This is why Paul speaks of a dispensation of grace.

> **Ephesians 3:2, 7-8** If ye have heard of the dispensation of the grace of God which is given me to you-ward: 7 Whereof I was made a minister, according to the gift of the grace of God given unto me by the effectual working of his power. 8 Unto me, who am less than the least of all saints, is this grace given, that I should preach among the Gentiles the unsearchable riches of Christ;

Paul says that his development as a minister to the Gentiles was a grace-oriented and regimented procedure. Generally God will progressively reveal the work of grace. The anointing of the Lord in your life will develop in this way.

> **Ephesians 4:7** But unto *everyone* of us is given grace according to the measure of the gift of Christ.

If we are to walk in the power and similitude of Christ, grace is essential. No person is exempt from this process. "Everyone" means every one.

How Do We Access Grace?

Grace can only be accessed by a devotion and love for the Heavenly Father.

> **Ephesians 1:6** To the praise of the glory of his grace, wherein he hath made us accepted in the beloved.

"In the beloved" should readily be translated in the *agape* or love of God. If we want to find grace, it will only be known as we dwell within the love of the Father.

This verse is very special as it possesses an extremely rare key to grace. The Greek word for **accepted** is *charitoo*. This word designates completed grace in a particular area. Another way of saying this is to say that we graduate into the objective of grace for that assigned pursuit. Whatever it was that God was requiring of us has been achieved, and we complete that phase of grace. The only other time that this derivative of grace can be found is in the Book of Luke.

> **Luke 1:28** And the angel came in unto her, and said, Hail, thou that art highly *favoured*, the

Lord is with thee: blessed art thou among women.

Of course, we recognize this passage as being the discourse between the archangel Gabriel and Mary, the mother of Jesus. When she is classified as being highly **favored**, *charitoo* is the Greek word that was chosen by God. The virtues present within the life of Mary made her the perfect choice for the service of God. These virtues came about as a result of her continued purity and chaste pursuit of God. Because of this lifestyle, God could utilize her in the ultimate point of service, becoming the mother of God. Our point of service will in some way reflect a birthing of Christ through us. God's completed grace will earmark our readiness for that great honor.

The Saints

7

Becoming A Son Of God

Sainthood is a theme that runs throughout the Word of God. It is central to the plan of God. The Holy Trinity works together in the pursuit of recruiting, training and implementing the saints. Jesus came to this planet in human form to suffer the death of the cross in order to redeem mankind back to the Father. Within that process our Lord patterned the walk of saintly living for all to see.

> **John 1:12** But as many as received him, to them gave he power to become the sons of God, even to them that believe on his name:

Whenever someone receives Jesus and believes on Him, they receive authority to become sons of God. Receiving Christ as Savior does not make you anything but a born-again baby. We have authority to "become," but authority needs to be accepted and accessed in order for it to function. Once we become the children of God, we've only initiated the possibility for development. This plan is not automatic and is generally not pursued by the majority of believers.

Jude provides a breakdown of the interplay of the Trinity in saintly development.

> **Jude 1** Jude, the servant of Jesus Christ, and brother of James, to them that are sanctified by God the Father, and preserved in Jesus Christ, and called.

The first influence Jude lists is "them," and he is talking about individuals. The process of saintly development must begin with each of us deciding to step into the sanctifying process of the Heavenly Father. This initiates the process of preserving or allowing Jesus to establish us in our place of service and livelihood. The Holy Ghost can then develop us according to call and commission. God has called each one of us, but it is our individual decision whether or not to accept that calling. When we determine that God means business with us and we commit to Him, the whole process of developing and sanctifying our lives is set in motion.

The Father sanctifies His people. Literally, we are "made to be holy or saintly" by virtue of our association with Him and by our ongoing obedience to His purposes and plans. The Father passionately desires for this to transpire, and he entrusts this process to the Holy Spirit. The word that is translated most often as saint in the New Testament is the same word that God uses to define His holiness, ***hagios***; therefore, the Holy Spirit could readily be called the Saintly Breath or Saintly Spirit.

JESUS: THE FIRSTBORN OF MANY SAINTS

When Jesus walked on the earth in physical form, the Saintly Spirit came upon Him and empowered the purpose of the

Heavenly Father through Him. Jesus patterned the ultimate in relationship with the Father and in demonstration of being a saint. He is the firstborn of many brethren, and before He ascended to heaven, Jesus asked the Father to send the saintly Comforter to us.

> **Acts 1:8** But ye shall receive power, after that the Holy Ghost is come upon you: and ye shall be witnesses unto me both in Jerusalem, and in all Judaea, and in Samaria, and unto the uttermost part of the earth.

When the Saintly Spirit comes upon us, we receive power as we become witnesses. A witness is a martyr or someone who dies to this life in order to serve the higher calling. This wonderful Saintly Spirit provides an abundance of grace to propel us through dimensions of change into new realms of promotion and operation. This is a saintly calling.

So we are given the authoritative right to become saints when we accept Jesus as Savior. God the Father lovingly commissions and oversees this "process of becoming," and the Holy Ghost empowers and accompanies the process.

> **Hebrews 12:2** Looking unto Jesus the author and finisher of our faith; who for the joy that was set before him endured the cross, despising the shame, and is set down at the right hand of the throne of God.

> **Romans 8:27** And he that searcheth the hearts knoweth what is the mind of the Spirit, because

he maketh intercession for the saints according to the will of God.

Our Lord Jesus is the one who has made this opportunity possible for us. He has devoted Himself to the will of the Father, and His intercession is the mighty gift of God to every saint. Jesus longs for the exact will of God to be transacted.

Within the next few chapters we take a closer look at this marvelous plan of God. We will see the mindset of our Heavenly Father as He displays His purpose for us. We were created for the purpose of knowing Him and revealing His presence and glory.

The Saints

The Saintly Operation of Our Heavenly Father

Our Father has a purpose for all things. He has a firm command of everything in this world, and His time-line is incorruptible. Interwoven into the ultimate purpose of God is the theme of saintly partnership with Him, of which He desires for everyone to be a part. God sent His Son, Jesus Christ, to ensure that opportunity. Whoever comes to Him will He in no wise cast out. God loved, and He sent His Son that "whosoever believes" might be saved (John 3:16). We are redeemed to the Father and not solely for eventual admittance into heaven.

GOD'S PURPOSE

We are told in the Bible that Lucifer, or Satan, was once a trusted and important part of the ministrations of heaven. When he rebelled in a failed heavenly coup, the position that he once held became vacated. God designed man to grow into and fulfill that vacated role. Adam and Eve were tempted by this fallen enemy and succumbed to a temptation that was disobedience to the Father's prime directive for them. Jesus came in order to restore the purpose of the Father for mankind. He accomplished that purpose.

Now God is culminating the process by mobilizing His people, the saints, to specifically partner with Him in defeating the remaining vestiges of rebellion within this planetary structure.

Every human being is predestined to participate in this program. Not one person is foreordained to fail; although, many will choose to neglect the callings of God. Some will even choose to fight on the side of the enemy in the war.

FROM THE FOUNDATION OF THE WORLD

There is perhaps no more important concept in the scriptures than that of predestination, and none which is more distorted and misunderstood. The enemy has caused millions of people to feel that God has no use for them and that somehow they do not figure into His divine plan. The reality is that God loves everyone and desires that all come to a saving knowledge of His Son.

The Heavenly Father desires that men and women partner with Him in the re-establishment of His Kingdom. Each person has a place in this plan if they so choose to accept God. No one is exempt from the merciful arms of the Father. Christianity wrestles in seemingly endless debate concerning who can and cannot be saved while the main theme of predestination is ignored. The main issue regarding predestination, or fore-ordination, regards the reason that man has been put on this globe. The theme is simply that God wants His planet back, and He desires to use men and women in partnership with angels to affect His plan. The wisdom of God regarding this extends to the time, which the Bible characterizes as the foundation of the world. A brief study of this phrase will illumine the topic of fore-ordination and the role of the saint within.

At the foundation of the world, God knew rebellion would visit His Kingdom and that a Redeemer must be provided. Jesus agreed to be the Redeemer so that those who accept Him would come to know the Father.

> **1 Peter 1:19-20** But with the precious blood of Christ, as of a lamb without blemish and without spot: 20 Who verily was foreordained before the foundation of the world, but was manifest in these last times for you,

> **Hebrews 9:26** Then Christ would have had to suffer many times since the creation of the world. But now he has appeared once for all at the end of the ages to do away with sin by the sacrifice of himself.

An acceptance of the Savior will provide right relationship with the Heavenly Father. It will also call us into a life of holiness or saintliness, in which we might walk in the pathway of the love of God. Being chosen is a classification denoting those that are actively in the service of the King according to saintly duty.

> **Ephesians 1:4** According as he hath chosen us in him before the foundation of the world, that we

should be holy and without blame before him in love:

Those who yield themselves to this walk will be granted prophetic vision from God as to how to move within this Kingdom principle. This is ably indicated in the Gospel of Matthew when the Father speaks to those who are on His right hand, which speaks of purpose.

> **Matthew 25:34** Then shall the King say unto them on his right hand, Come, ye blessed of my Father, inherit the kingdom prepared for you from the foundation of the world:

The understanding of the things of the Kingdom will not be easily discerned by the natural mind. The Lord Jesus will reveal these things to those who are entirely dedicated to the cause of the Father. The mysteries of the Kingdom have been reserved from the foundation of the world and will be shown forth in parables, dreams and visions.

> **Matthew 13:35** That it might be fulfilled which was spoken by the prophet, saying, I will open my mouth in parables; I will utter things which have been kept secret from the foundation of the world.

The process through which predestination is revealed in us will vary from person to person; however, there are many constants that are endemic to the process and are readily found within the Word of God.

God has hidden His ways of progressive revelation. He has also hidden His servants in order that they might be revealed in the hour of their destiny. These two are integrally linked together within the framework of God's heart.

PROGRESSION OF PREDESTINATION

> **Romans 8:28-33** And we know that all things work together for good to them that love God, to them who are the called according to his purpose. 29 For whom he did foreknow, he also did predestinate to be conformed to the image of his Son, that he might be the firstborn among many brethren. 30 Moreover whom he did predestinate, them he also called: and whom he called, them he also justified: and whom he justified, them he also glorified. 31 What shall we then say to these things? If God be for us, who can be against us? 32 He that spared not his own Son, but delivered him up for us all, how shall he not with him also freely give us all things? 33 Who shall lay any thing to the charge of God's elect? It is God that justifieth.

God has a purpose, and He calls everyone to fulfill that purpose. Within this dynamic passage observe the familiar progression: Love of the Father; purpose and foreknowledge of God; predestination and calling of the saints; justifying or becoming conformable to and within the example of Jesus; glorification of God and the participation within the demonstration of His glory.

This is why God created us. He did not create us solely to get us "saved" in order that we might then sit on a pew and wait for the rapture. He created us to pursue Him and to dwell in His Love. God does not tell us that all things will work out for us just because we are saved. God tells us that if we are seeking His heart, pressing into His love because we are called for a purpose, THEN all things will work together for us. The price that we pay in order to enjoy this realm of blessing is to pursue God passionately.

God made us for a reason, and there is only one true course for us. We are predestined to do what God wants in patterning our lives after Jesus. Even at the age of 12, Jesus was about His Father's business because He was predestined for that purpose. We are made for this pattern of prayer and seeking after the Father and doing things that might seem unusual but are redemptive and instructive.

An interchangeable word for justification is righteousness. God's righteousness is His established purpose on this planet and in our life. When righteousness is fairly won by willingness and obedience to the Lord, the enemy is defeated and the glory of the

Lord is revealed. The glory of the Lord will be upon us as the culmination of grace, or promotion, is realized.

> **Ephesians 1:4-6** According as he hath chosen us in him before the foundation of the world, that we should be holy and without blame before him in love: 5 Having predestinated us unto the adoption of children by Jesus Christ to himself, according to the good pleasure of his will, 6 To the praise of the glory of his grace, wherein he hath made us accepted in the beloved.

SANCTIFICATION BY THE FATHER

> **Jude 1** Jude, the servant of Jesus Christ, and brother of James, to them that are sanctified by God the Father, and preserved in Jesus Christ, and called.

The Father longs for us to be sanctified or holy. The word translated as **sanctified** is *hagios*, which is the same word used for **holy** many times throughout the New Testament. Many have a twisted perception of sanctification or holiness and view it as a long list of "dos and don'ts." The word here actually means "to make holy, to purify or consecrate." When God calls us and sanctifies us, He is calling us to His fullness. This means that if we will surrender ourselves to what God wants to do, there will be no limit to what He can do in us.

The fullness of the Father is available to us because He wants us to be abundantly blessed. He wants us to succeed and gain access to every available gifting. He sanctifies us because He does not want us to be mediocre representatives of His Kingdom. He has prepared things for us that are dynamic in scope and measure, and there are no limits to the realm of our success when we truly yield ourselves to His process of sanctification.

MANY CALLED, FEW CHOSEN

God tells us in many passages of scripture that we are called, we are invited, and we are appointed to be very special in Him. Each of us is born into this world with specific significance to the Kingdom of God. We need to accept this calling that God has given us and move forward in the progression of being "chosen." Jesus teaches about the Father's development of His saints in two different passages.

- **In His Majesty's Service**

    Matthew 20:16 So the last shall be first, and the first last: for many be called, but few chosen.

In this passage Jesus is talking about the fields and vineyards where some came and worked at the beginning of the day for an agreed upon wage. Others came at the last hour and worked and received the same wage as those that had worked all day. Those who were there from the beginning complained because the newcomers received the same wages. The Lord of the Harvest responds that the original agreement was equitable. He then concludes the argument with "for many are called, but few chosen."

The Lord stresses the great significance of those who come into the field at the end. They are not more important than those who had been there throughout the day, but they are essential to getting the job done. They are not met with great delight by the tenured laborers within the field. God has gifted many as prodigies that possess great talents and passions. He is calling them unto Him and is attempting to move them from the process of calling into that which signifies choosing or commissioning.

The church is known in the New Testament as *ekklesia*, or ones drawn out from the world. The word for **called** in this passage is the word *kletos*, or those that are invited to something fresh and appealing. **Chosen** is the Greek word *eklektos*, which means those that are favorites or preferred.

We perceive that the church is drawn out from the mire of the sin of this world. God then desires for the redeemed to begin to develop into the sons that can know and serve Him mightily, and so he calls them into something fresh and new. If these called ones respond with obedient desire, they move into the category of being the favorites of God, or the chosen ones.

Those that the Father adds to the vineyard must be accepted with love, and they should graciously be welcomed into the fields of service. It is imperative that the established servants continue to flow in humility before the Father in passionate obedience.

- **In His Majesty's Mantle**

   Matthew 22:14 For many are called, but few are chosen.

In this passage Jesus is talking about a wedding feast that is being prepared at this time. The lord of that feast passes through and perceives someone sitting without a proper wedding garment. He responds in a manner that is rather harsh. He has the guest bound hand and foot and cast into outer darkness. It is at this point that Jesus declares, "many are called, but few are chosen."

This startling account reminds us of the necessity of remaining current within the ongoing processes of the Lord. The context of this passage speaks of the good and the bad being welcomed to the feast. The man was speechless, which implies an absence of ongoing communication with the Father. There is a great likelihood that this man was an enemy representative who was subsequently cast into outer darkness. His missing wedding garment was the white linen of the saints.

GIFTS AND CALLINGS OF THE FATHER

> **Romans 11:26-29** And so all Israel shall be saved: as it is written, There shall come out of Sion the Deliverer, and shall turn away ungodliness from Jacob: 27 For this is my covenant unto them, when I shall take away their sins. 28 As concerning the gospel, they are enemies for your sakes: but as touching the election, they are beloved for the fathers' sakes. 29 For the gifts and calling of God are without repentance.

This passage speaks of Israel and the church; and while the role of Israel in this process is not the theme of this book, the principle outlined remains consistent with the process proclaimed in this chapter. Within the framework of our discussion, God offers gifts, or "graces," to everyone. These are His anointed opportunities for advancement. The concept of the people of Israel is vital to this discussion as they were not faithful to the calling of God. Furthermore, what they knew about God prohibited them from stepping into His ultimate revelation through Jesus.

This startling reality should serve as a vivid warning to us. If God would divorce Israel and prune them during the inception of the church, how much more would the grafted branch need to abide faithful to Him and His ways? We must be what God calls us to be or He will find someone else to do His bidding.

> **2 Timothy 1:9** Who hath saved us, and called us with an holy calling, not according to our works, but according to his own purpose and grace, which was given us in Christ Jesus before the world began.

We are saved and invited to a holy, or saintly, mission according to God's purpose that was foreknown before the world began. Christ Jesus patterned and empowered this process of becoming, and it is solely by the force of His promotional grace that we develop.

> **2 Peter 1:10** Wherefore the rather, brethren, give diligence to make your calling and election sure: for if ye do these things, ye shall never fall:

Peter, the headstrong one, comments upon this reality by stating that we must guard over the calling of the Father and our ultimate fulfillment of that calling. We must make it a surety as it is not something to take lightly. We must "earnestly contend for the faith once delivered to the saints" (Jude 3).

...AND FAITHFUL

> **Revelation 17:14** These shall make war with the Lamb, and the Lamb shall overcome them: for he is Lord of lords, and King of kings: and

they that are with him are called, and chosen, and faithful.

In the Book of Revelation, a final facet is added to the equation for those who abide to the end. These are not only designated as being called and chosen, but faithful. Faithfulness is a key ingredient to the saintly walk. The first sign of the apostolic is patience, and that requires faithfulness.

> **2 Corinthians 12:12** Truly the signs of an apostle were wrought among you in all patience, in signs, and wonders, and mighty deeds.

It will not be the signs, wonders or mighty deeds that keep these saints. It will be their faithful adherence to the establishment of God's purpose within and through them. Remember that the Lord will say to these ones on the great Day of Judgment, "Well done, thou good and faithful servant" (Matthew 25:23).

Even after we have attained the called and chosen levels, we must continue to be faithful and press forward. We must be willing to resist what comes against us and never abandon the mandate of God's leading. We must be faithful to the Lord in our passions, in our prayer, devotion, worship, study and obedience.

We will be tempted to simply abide within the new realms into which we have moved in the Lord, especially since each progression has been wrought by virtue of much sacrifice and war on our part. The Bible says that our Great Shepherd leads us by the still waters, and we feed in the lush grasses (Psalm 23:1-3). But the Shepherd at some point tells the sheep it is time to get up and keep moving. Our Shepherd wants a people who, no matter how good and lush the place to which He has led, will keep moving ahead in Him.

It is often difficult to get people who are in the "called" state to move into the cost of the "chosen" state, especially if they do not want to move. It is equally difficult to get people who are in the "chosen" level to move into that place of "faithfulness" because of the temptation to find a comfortable place and dwell on that plateau. If we are at a comfortable place, why do we need to keep moving? Those that are with Jesus are not only called and chosen but are faithful to move with Him wherever He is going.

A NATION OF SAINTS

> **1 Peter 2:9** But ye are a chosen generation, a royal priesthood, an holy nation, a peculiar people; that ye should shew forth the praises of him who hath called you out of darkness into his marvellous light.

There is a move of God in each generation. The day in which we live affords a greater move than has yet been known on this globe. Those who cooperate with God in His calling will comprise a chosen generation for this last hour.

There will be those who operate in a priestly function. They will be kings in the spirit realm of whom Jesus is the ultimate King. They will comprise a nation of saints, a people who are ambassadors of heaven. This will truly be a peculiarity, even to the church in general. God will use them to shine as lights in the darkness. How thrilling!

In many parables, the Lord Jesus spoke of people that were entrusted with talents and stewardship of lands. Invariably, as these people were faithful in their service to God, they were promoted. Consider this example:

> **Matthew 25:23** His lord said unto him, Well done, good and faithful servant; thou hast been faithful over a few things, I will make thee ruler over many things: enter thou into the joy of thy lord.

God will reward His servants according to their faithfulness and according to their fulfillment of His required service. Ultimately, the ranking of kings and lords will be dependent upon how God views the services of those to whom He has entrusted much responsibility.

Each new challenge prompts a new opportunity to know and love the Heavenly Father. Knowing God intimately is the key factor in service and promotion. Within the framework of the parable just cited, an unfaithful servant was also described. Perhaps the most telling commentary that he offered was this:

> **Matthew 25:24** Then he which had received the one talent came and said, Lord, I knew thee that thou art an hard man...

This individual had obviously known God in the past or he would never have been entrusted with the talent that was given him. He had known God but did not presently know Him. This is what caused the unfaithful steward to fail. We must know God in the now regardless of how much we have known Him in our past successes.

Knowing God is the key to everything in the walk of the saints just as it is in all other areas of our existence.

The Saints

The Saintly Influence of The Holy Spirit

Jesus said that when He ascended to His Father, He would ask for the Father to send the Comforter to His people. This Comforter is the Holy Spirit, and His name means the one called alongside to help us. With the help of the Holy Spirit, we will do the same works and even greater works than those of Jesus.

> **John 14:12** Verily, verily, I say unto you, He that believeth on me, the works that I do shall he do also; and greater works than these shall he do; because I go unto my Father.

The word translated as **greater** is *meizon*. It implies numerical superiority as well as improvement in quality of the work. There are things that the Heavenly Father has preserved for this hour that will absolutely amaze and captivate the heart of His people. The Holy Spirit is the driving life and strength of this course of action.

When we talk of the Holy Spirit, we could quite literally call Him the "saintly wind" or saintly breath of God. When God breathed life into man, Adam became a living spirit. When the sound of the rushing mighty wind came upon the church on the day of Pentecost, the church was born by the wind of God.

> **Jude 1** Jude, the servant of Jesus Christ, and brother of James, to them that are sanctified by God the Father, and preserved in Jesus Christ, and called.

Implied within this verse is the role of the Holy Spirit in the life of the saint. Truly, He is the operational force of God in the process of developing us into the people that we are purposed to become. His role as the Comforter, or one called alongside to help, is a role of equipping and supervising our development as saints. Many are called, but few allow for this process to be actualized within them.

> **John 16:13** Howbeit when he, the Spirit of truth, is come, he will guide you into all truth: for he shall not speak of himself; but whatsoever he shall hear, that shall he speak: and he will shew you things to come.

Herein is a picture of the absolute devotion of the Holy Spirit to the purpose of the Father. John declares that the Holy Ghost will teach us the truths of God's unfolding plan so that we might be equipped to operate as proficient agents of our Heavenly Father. This is a selfless action, and it patterns a mode of selflessness that must be the guiding force of every saint. If God Himself in the person of the Holy Spirit will not vary from the purpose of righteousness, we must also humble ourselves for the same cause.

SPIRITUAL GIFTS AND SAINTLY WINDS

There is a difference between this saintly wind of sanctifying that is essential to saintly development and the gifts of the Spirit (1 Corinthians 12). The showing forth of the Spirit in ***charismata***, or grace gifts, is simply what the name implies. ***Charismata***, or with grace, speaks of the way that God elevates people from one place to another. When we were born again, grace caught us up from the depth of sin and placed us into right standing with God. Salvation encompasses any place from which we are in need of deliverance or revelation. Grace lifts us into the position of freedom or promotion. Grace gifts come to elevate the recipient into a new territory of victory, sometimes within the realm of promotion, and often as a turning point in intercessory warfare.

By their very name, the grace gifts are for the purpose of promotion into new levels of service and relationship with God. This will require a maturity on behalf of the recipient because it involves constant development and change. Remember that the Holy Spirit comes for the purpose of developing us in truth and to continually show us the next thing to come. There is little time for stationary existence, and no place for prideful assessment of how far we have progressed. Grace gifts move us forward and remind us of the words of the Apostle Paul concerning pressing on and forgetting that which is behind.

GROANINGS OF THE HOLY SPIRIT

> **Romans 8:26** Likewise the Spirit also helpeth our infirmities: for we know not what we should pray for as we ought: but the Spirit itself maketh intercession for us with groanings which cannot be uttered.

This passage is generally relegated to the thought of the Spirit of God helping us when we are absolutely bereft of strength and understanding. It feels good when you are hurting to rely on the Holy Ghost to pray through you to work everything out. Although this is a truth that many have relied upon in times of trouble, it is not the main emphasis within the context of this chapter. We must move from the milk-level understanding and proceed to a deeper level of understanding.

It is rather simplistic to believe that the God of all creation could only muster within us an unutterable noise. The groaning of the Spirit is prolific, usually marking an opportunity of great importance. Think of this for a moment. Just as mankind when faced with a seemingly insurmountable task will express the exasperated cry of essential energy, so the Spirit of the Lord will step in and express the heart cry of the Father. This generally happens at times of crucial significance. Let us examine two such examples in the New Testament.

- **For The Development of the Disciples**

    John 11:38-39 Jesus therefore again groaning in himself cometh to the grave. It was a cave, and a stone lay upon it. 39 Jesus said, Take ye away the stone.

Our Lord Jesus groaned in the midst of a vital opportunity to show forth the mighty power of God. The Holy Spirit within Him registered not only the obvious need of the moment for the raising of the dead but also something far more important for the future needs of His disciples. Jesus was focusing on the reaction and perceptions of His followers, and He registered this as being a key moment of development for them.

Grasp this truth, as it is imperative toward perceiving God's heart. Within this framework that included facing the grief of His friends, and with the prospect of a pending miracle before Him, the concern of the Lord Jesus was upon the central reaction and perception of His followers. Of all the demanding factors found within this episode, the one that produced a groaning within the heart of God was the aspect that involved the development of the disciples.

- **For The Redemption Of The Earth**

Creation groaningly awaits the culmination of the redemption of the earth. The same Holy Spirit who brooded upon the face of the deep of the pre-Adamic world is still moving upon this planet. This created place yearns for the saint and for the eventual deliverance from the cycle of defeat and cursed existence.

> **Romans 8:22** For we know that the whole creation groaneth and travaileth in pain together until now.

When the Spirit of the living God groans within us, it is not an indication that He is speechless. The groaning of the Spirit works to overcome the things that have been hindering us from transitioning. He works to break through the walls holding us back from the mysteries of the Lord. The Spirit works to open us up to the purposes that God originally intended for us and for this planet.

His ministry is to prepare a bride to rule and reign beside Jesus as a partner in the heavens and on this earth. The work of the Holy Ghost is to engender our devotion to the Lord Jesus, to draw us to the Father and to infuse us with power. He protects us and draws us to divine encounters. He is the wonderful influence that empowers us to do the things Jesus and the Father command.

The Lord Jesus in Saintly Development

Our Lord Jesus embodies the most pivotal role in the maturation of the saints. He is the firstborn of many brethren. He not only pioneered the walk but also oversees the saint unto perfection.

> **John 6:44** No man can come to me, except the Father which hath sent me draw him: and I will raise him up at the last day.
>
> **John 15:16** Ye have not chosen me, but I have chosen you, and ordained you, that ye should go and bring forth fruit, and that your fruit should remain: that whatsoever ye shall ask of the Father in my name, he may give it you.

We must recognize that God created each person for the purpose of serving Him. Throughout the course of our life, God continually calls to us. He draws us to a place of purpose, and it is our responsibility to accept and welcome that calling. Jesus is called the firstborn of many brethren, and He came to the earth for the purpose of opening this opportunity for us to know His Father.

For those that accept this calling, there will subsequently be a leading into a place of productivity and fruit bearing. The place where you are planted is a terrain of God's Kingdom that you have been destined to develop.

TEREO

> **Jude 1** Jude, the servant of Jesus Christ, and brother of James, to them that are sanctified by God the Father, and **preserved** in Jesus Christ, and called.

Jude speaks of the preserving ministry of Jesus which is translated from the Greek word *tereo*. This word has many unique meanings, but the predominate definition is that of a territory or site acquired and maintained in proper rule and authority. We are called of the Father to establish the Kingdom where He leads and places us. Jesus will cover us there and establish our ways. For this purpose Jesus gives gifts of procuring and establishing for the perfecting of the saints.

> **Ephesians 4:11-12** And he gave some, apostles; and some, prophets; and some, evangelists; and some, pastors and teachers; 12 For the perfecting of the saints, for the work of the ministry, for the edifying of the body of Christ:

INTERCESSION

> **Hebrews 7:25-26** Wherefore he is able also to save them to the uttermost that come unto God by him, seeing he ever liveth to make intercession for them. 26 For such an high priest became us, who is holy, harmless, undefiled,

separate from sinners, and made higher than the heavens;

Our great intercessor invests His heart into the ministry of intercession. Our great High Priest ever lives to intercede for those who come to the Father. The most necessary attribute that someone could present to the Father is a desire to know Him and do His bidding. We are told that He is first and foremost committed to the holy, or saintly.

> **Romans 8:27** And he that searcheth the hearts knoweth what is the mind of the Spirit, because he maketh intercession for the saints according to the will of God.

The Scriptures identify the one who searches the hearts as being our Lord Jesus. His emphasis of intercession before the throne is on behalf of the Father's purpose, which is what He came to the earth to fulfill. Jesus is cooperating with the Holy Ghost as they seek together to bring the saints into alignment with the Father's business. He is praying for the saints to rise up and fulfill this calling.

> **John 17:9** I pray for them: I pray not for the world, but for them which thou hast given me; for they are thine.

Many people assume that Jesus is praying for the lost, but a close study of the scriptures reveals a different truth. Jesus told his disciples shortly before His death that He was praying for those whom God had given Him. Jesus is praying for those who are moving up in the Father into a place of standing with Him. He is praying for God's purposes to be revealed in the saints.

To Know The Father

> **John 17:19-22** And for their sakes I sanctify myself, that they also might be sanctified through the truth. 20 Neither pray I for these alone, but for them also which shall believe on me through their word; 21 That they all may be one; as thou, Father, art in me, and I in thee, that they also may be one in us: that the world may believe that thou hast sent me. 22 And the glory which thou gavest me I have given them; that they may be one, even as we are one:

Jesus is praying here for the company of His beloved. He is also praying for those that are touched by the impact of the beloved. The primary emphasis for all of them is that they might be recipients of the same glory that Jesus knew in the Father and that they might become one with the Father. This is an exchange within the realm of *agape*.

Many believers only relate to God in the soulish or emotional realm. Some relate in the *eros*, or fleshly realm, as they are only interested in having their earthly desires met. Some are only waiting for an eventual union in the sweet bye and bye.

However, Jesus demonstrated a oneness with the Father while on earth and was longing for that same unity for His disciples. A candid observance of the church world today will reveal that this type of pursuit is not currently widespread. There is a difference between accepting Christ as Savior and making Him Lord.

TO ADHERE TO HIS PURPOSES

What exactly does our Lord Jesus pray? He is the Chief Intercessor of the saints, and He is ultimately devoted to the task of getting us ready to serve the Father more efficiently. This prayer is a pattern for us and speaks of the necessity of the place of strong commune with the Father in our life.

Jesus wants us to be fulfilled in our service to Him. He is not praying for your late car payment or for Aunt Edith's bunion. In fact, He told us that in the day in which we live we would ask Him for nothing.

> **John 16:23** And in that day ye shall ask me nothing. Verily, verily, I say unto you, Whatsoever ye shall ask the Father in my name, he will give it you.

If we are not to ask Jesus for the provision of the cares of life, why do we in any way assume that He is praying about those things? His aspirations are set on a much higher goal – the saintly calling upon your life. The Lord desires for you to advance in the changing process that transforms you from glory to glory according to the perfect will of the Father.

Nowhere is the prayer ministry of the Lord more pronounced than in His relationship with Peter. Jesus knew that Peter was going to face great hurdles in relationship to the attack of the enemy. Note the manner in which Jesus counsels him.

> **Luke 22:31-32** And the Lord said, Simon, Simon, behold, Satan hath desired to have you, that he may sift you as wheat: 32 But I have prayed for thee, that thy faith fail not: and when thou art converted, strengthen thy brethren.

SPRINKLING OF THE BLOOD

> **1 Peter 1:2** Elect according to the foreknowledge of God the Father, through sanctification of the Spirit, unto obedience and sprinkling of the blood of Jesus Christ: Grace unto you, and peace, be multiplied.

Peter, perhaps the most brash of all of Christ's disciples, speaks of his experience within the process of development as a saint. Of all of the disciples, Peter serves as the most prolific example of dying to self. His natural passions were immense, and they often subjected him to grave predicaments. However, the process of saintly development was achieved in his life. There is clearly a four-fold progression within this course of sainthood that culminates with the sprinkling of the blood of the Lamb.

The first step in this progression is the foreknowledge of the Father, which is the same predestination spoken of in Jude 1. We must first know that we have been chosen and that God has a plan for us.

He next mentions the ***hagiosmos*** of the Spirit or the "making saintly" dynamic of God through the Holy Spirit. Paul speaks of this same principle when he tells us we are chosen by the Father to be part of the process of "sanctification of the Spirit and the belief of the truth." This leads to the "obtaining of the glory of our Lord Jesus Christ" (2 Thessalonians 2:13-14).

Once again, this sanctification is not designed by God to engender a "wringing of the hands" regarding sin in your life. This process involves submitting your sails to the wind of the Spirit and become so captivated in your heart by the Lord that there is not room for anything else but Him. You become apprehended so that you lose the desire for anything but the Lord. Once captivated by that love, you then must be willing to submit to His processes. This is where many cease to move forward.

Peter next says that obedience to the process, or adherence to Godly influences of change, is paramount to the success of

God's plan. If there are parts of us in the sanctifying process that are unwilling to yield to the Spirit, then obedience is a difficult thing. Obedience involves our making a choice to do something that the Lord wants rather than what we want to do. We must allow the Lord to train our ears to hear His words so that we are able to obey.

The last step in the progression is of astonishing significance; that is, the sprinkling of the blood. Levitical purposes and directives for the sprinkling of blood are amply defined in many Biblical commentaries. In the process of saintly development we ascertain many appropriately powerful insights involved with the sprinkling of the blood.

- **Better Than That Of Abel**

    Hebrews 12:24 And to Jesus the mediator of the new covenant, and to the blood of sprinkling, that speaketh better things than that of Abel.

If the blood of Abel cried out from the ground to the Heavenly Father, how much more does the blood of our Lord Jesus speak from the ground as a testament of ownership and establishment?

What message would the blood of Jesus cry out from the ground? Undoubtedly, it cries out the fact that the earth is the Lord's and the fullness thereof. This entire globe is the *tereos* of the Father. Jesus is absolutely intent on this planet being returned to its rightful owner and becoming once again the place of worship to the Father.

- **Worship**

Abel offered a sacrifice of obedience that was pleasing to God. The story of the murder of Abel tells us that he offered praise to the Lord that was not readily accepted by others who were also commanded to worship. This engendered anger and a murderous intent (Genesis 4). The majority of general believers will not readily accept true saints. Like Cain, many within the general church prefer to offer to God what is pleasing to themselves and convenient. They cannot tolerate someone from within the family who breaks traditional mindsets and does something different from what they do.

Cain-minded individuals also want a bloodless worship. They do not want anything that will cost their life and prefer to give something that is the fruit of their labor; however, God always demands a living sacrifice.

Most worship services are designed to meet the needs of people and ease the weary minds of those in attendance. Most prayer meetings are an exercise in airing shopping lists to God. Like the foolish virgins, many within the church are interested in what God can give to them as opposed to what they can give to Him. For the saint, worship and prayer are a matter of serving God rather than their own interests.

God wants us to return to ground level worship and prayer. When you worship you serve God in His way. When you pray you submit your life to God for His directive. After you have sought Him first, then all of the other things will be added unto you.

Another powerful dimension of the power of the sprinkling of the Blood is found within God's counsel to Cain. In the midst of their discussion regarding worship and sacrifice, God speaks of the door that leads to Him.

> **Genesis 4:7** If thou doest well, shalt thou not be accepted? and if thou doest not well, sin lieth at the door. And unto thee shall be his desire, and thou shalt rule over him.

Outside that doorway, or portal of access, sin is said to be crouching. God says that this sin will feed upon our desires, but that we have the capacity to overcome and rule over the darkness. It is imperative that every worshipper recognize this unwavering truth. Sin crouches at the door of every access point leading to God. We will only survive its onslaught when we are cleansed by the blood of the Lamb and refuse to entertain the thoughts of the natural mind.

Thoughts of jealousy, lust, competition, self and a myriad of others will be immediately targeted by the adversary. If we do not have clean hands and a pure heart, we will not be able to come through the doorway to the Father in worship. Our lips may praise, but our heart will be far from the Lord in a place of open defiance. The Bible tells of the importance of being cleansed by the blood of sprinkling, and it is imperative that we heed this wise and indelible counsel.

- **Cleansing And Purging**

    Hebrews 10:22 Let us draw near with a true heart in full assurance of faith, having our hearts sprinkled from an evil conscience, and our bodies washed with pure water.

    Hebrews 9:14 How much more shall the blood of Christ, who through the eternal Spirit offered himself without spot to God, purge your conscience from dead works to serve the living God?

Our conscience can be an evil thing. We have the capacity to entertain thoughts that are disgusting. Perhaps the most distasteful of errors that our minds can conjure is that of self-righteousness. Like Cain, it does not matter to God what we think is acceptable to Him. It only matters what God wants.

The Holy Spirit is trying to do a work in our heart and in our spirits. There may be an iniquity within us that is bent; a conscience of evil that attempts to wrest control of our belief system and our passion. The Bible says "the evil conscience of the heart" not of the mind. If there is an evil conscience that wages war and gains control of your heart, it can prevent the work that the Spirit is trying to perform.

The Word of God tells us that sin stemming from the sins of the father can be passed onto the third and fourth generations. Some families are stronger in a spiritual dimension, and the enemy usually attacks that aspect of strength. If you have come into a deeper walk with God and entered into the process of saintly development, you need to receive a fresh sprinkling of the blood to purge the evil conscience that would attempt to resurrect generational strongholds.

Some scholars assert that there is no difference between sin and iniquity. This contention does not bear witness with the close scrutiny of scripture as there are continual references to both sin and iniquity. Iniquity will lead to sin as the twisting of behavioral pattern will regularly cause us to miss the mark of God in our activities.

Our mind needs a fresh sprinkling of the blood of Christ on a daily basis. God wants to enliven our ability to understand the things of His Holy Word. He desires to show us things in the scriptures that we have never seen before. He wants to loosen some of our interpretations that are literally comprised of the traditions of men and give to us a drink of the new wine of revelation.

Many are convinced that they would be the first to know if they had a problem. The blood goes where we may not be able to reach or even be aware. The word "sprinkling" gives a very picturesque image as it is sporadic and unpredictable in application. If you were to sprinkle several pieces of paper with paint, you would gain a new pattern of application on each page. The Holy Ghost uses this word in order to depict the specialized cleansing of the Spirit of God. Each person is different, and each point of necessity will differ from the last. God knows exactly where the cleansing needs to be applied. We do not need to be "born again" over and over again as that is a washing. Sprinkling is remedial care, orchestrated by the Spirit of God.

- **Sprinkling Brings Revelation**

    Hebrews 9:19-21 For when Moses had spoken every precept to all the people according to the law, he took the blood of calves and of goats, with water, and scarlet wool, and hyssop, and sprinkled both the book, and all the people, 20 Saying, This is the blood of the testament which God hath enjoined unto you. 21 Moreover he sprinkled with blood both the tabernacle, and all the vessels of the ministry.

Moses sprinkled the book and all the people. He also sprinkled the tabernacle and all the vessels of ministry. We must be cognizant of the fact that God wants to use this body of ours. He classifies it as the Temple of the Holy Ghost. Like the Mercy Seat being sprinkled, God wants to meet with us in His fresh presence. He wants to visit us with new mercies and wants to reveal grace to us in ways that we have never known. Our carnal ability to perceive must be sprinkled by the blood of the Lamb in order to see as God sees.

LIFE-GIVING BLOOD

There is never anything ordinary about the blood of Christ. The issues that have just been mentioned can become ordinary if we allow them to be so.

Whenever we encounter the blood of Jesus, a life-giving transaction occurs. When we are born again, we receive the gift of eternal life through His sacrifice. Each time the blood of sprinkling is applied, we are supplied with a unique capacity of the life of our Lord. Purification for our most present opportunity of service or development is essential for success. The blood serves to equip and propel us in ways that nothing else can match. In essence, its adoptive measure triggers the release of grace and mercy, and we are launched into places that we could never hope to gain through our own energy or merit.

As we are changed from glory to glory, the sprinkling of the blood brings us a life-giving impetus. We are born into the changes that God leads us to experience. We die daily and live afresh to God. The blood of sprinkling accomplishes this miracle. We overcome the enemy forces of this hour by yielding our life to the Lord, receiving fresh revelation from His mouth and by the blood of the Lamb (Revelation 12:11). Undoubtedly, the blood of sprinkling is a mighty dimension of this overcoming process.

The Developmental Stages Of The Saints

Born-again believers in Jesus Christ are members of the family of God, but they may never ascend beyond the classification of a general family member. God cannot entrust His power and the privilege of partnership to those who dwell in a non-expectant state of existence.

BECOMING A SON OF GOD

> **Galatians 4:1-7** Now I say, That the heir, as long as he is a child, differeth nothing from a servant, though he be lord of all; 2 But is under tutors and governors until the time appointed of the father. 3 Even so we, when we were children, were in bondage under the elements of the world: 4 But when the fulness of the time was come, God sent forth his Son, made of a woman, made under the law, 5 To redeem them that were under the law, that we might receive the adoption of sons. 6 And because ye are sons, God hath sent forth the Spirit of his Son into your hearts, crying, Abba, Father. 7 Wherefore thou art no more a servant, but a son; and if a son, then an heir of God through Christ.

The family progression is of vital importance. Some believers enter the family of God and then choose to abide in passive state. They do not develop a deeper understanding of God but instead live in fear and bondage to the trends of the Christian world. Only knowing things taught to them by somebody else, they become enslaved to those mindsets. They gravitate toward various waves of teaching and want to be told what to believe, think and say. God has called them to be sons, and this powerful provision resides within each child of God.

POWER TO BECOME

> **John 1:12** But as many as received him, to them gave he power to become the sons of God, even to them that believe on his name:

Jesus gave to those who believe on Him the power to become sons of God. Power to become something is far different than actually being that something.

> **Romans 8:14** For as many as are led by the Spirit of God, they are the sons of God.

We are told that in order to be called sons of God we have to be led by the Spirit of God. The word used for led is always used to define a person or possession in the control of someone else. This is different from simply receiving a gift of the Spirit or a word from the Spirit. To be led by the Spirit is to be continually directed in lifestyle and development. At His ascension Jesus promised that power would come upon the disciples. It was power to be a witness, the power to learn to die to self.

SAINTLY DEVELOPMENT

> **1 John 3:1-3** Behold, what manner of love the Father hath bestowed upon us, that we should be called the sons of God: therefore the world knoweth us not, because it knew him not. 2 Beloved, now are we the sons of God, and it doth not yet appear what we shall be: but we know that, when he shall appear, we shall be like him; for we shall see him as he is. 3 And every man that hath this hope in him purifieth himself, even as he is pure.

John equates being a son of God to the process of being changed. He further states that to be in the process we must continually submit ourselves to purifying or becoming saintly – *hagnizo*. One of the prime aspects of being perfected as a saint is that we will not be understood by the world. The modern trend of making the church appealing to the outside world is a phenomenon that does not readily align with the teachings of the Bible. Many churches are so much like the world that it is more akin to joining a country club. Appealing is the watchword, and there is little talk about the sacrifice of growing in God.

The Apostle says that the sons of God dwell continually in a state of construction. When he says that it does not yet appear what we shall be, he means just that! We can walk into any Christian bookstore and locate volumes that have been written for the sole purpose of telling the child of God what he or she should be, think and do.

Further, the writer to the Hebrews speaks of a chastening influence that is necessary if we are to be counted as sons of God.

> **Hebrews 12:7-8** If ye endure chastening, God dealeth with you as with sons; for what son is he whom the father chasteneth not? 8 But if ye be without chastisement, whereof all are partakers, then are ye bastards, and not sons.

Paul informs us that to become a son of God, we must endure God's chastening. No matter which way you slice the word "chastening," it still feels the same. A child without chastening is called a bastard in the Word of God, but a son will endure chastening.

What is chastening anyway? Is it cruel and unusual suffering and discipline or some hardhearted mode of relationship with an uncaring guardian? No, of course, God is not this way. Chastening is an act geared toward God's refining and purifying process. It is always bordered by an intense love and closeness from the heart of our Father in Heaven.

Truly, to endure means to participate in all phases of the procedure. It costs something to become a son. It costs your very life.

HEIRS AND JOINT HEIRS

> **Romans 8:17** And if children, then heirs; heirs of God, and joint-heirs with Christ; if so be that we suffer with him, that we may be also glorified together.

Throughout this process the Father entrusts us with graduated responsibility. As we seek Him and flow in obedience, we are placed in areas of greater responsibility. Accordingly, the issue of suffering is included in this progression from heir to joint-heir. Our Lord learned obedience through the things that He suffered.

> **Hebrews 5:8** Though he were a Son, yet learned he obedience by the things which he suffered

Obedience is paramount to the process of promotion in God. This is essential to any sequence of higher development. The suffering mentioned is not suffering that is brought about because of disobedience or involvement in the wages of sin or willful ignorance. Rather, it is suffering for the purposes of God that will come because of the dying of self or the opposition of the enemy.

SUFFERING WITHIN THE PROCESS

The acceptance of the plan of God in your life will not win many friends for you on this earth. You might be opposed by the world, by your family, and even by the church.

> **Matthew 21:38** But when the husbandmen saw the son, they said among themselves, This is the heir; come, let us kill him, and let us seize on his inheritance.

Those who represent their Father will be opposed violently by the world. The Kingdom suffers violence, and the people of God must yield themselves to violent obedience to God. We must be willing to exert whatever influence is necessary in order for our task to be accomplished. Rest assured that the enemies of this world know that their time is short so they resist defeat with immense effort and resolve. It is often a question of who really wants the prize more – the invader or the occupational force.

Jesus came to engender warfare for this planet and for the souls of men and women. He did not come promising peace without battle. The enemy will mobilize any and all forces that will serve his purpose of resisting the movement of the saints. He will stop at nothing in his attempts to stop you.

This mission is what Jesus specified as the "Gospel of the Kingdom." We preach the Kingdom of God as Christ did in His ministry before the cross. In a prolific treatise concerning the end times, Christ Jesus spoke of many things that would come about in the final hours of the world. He then makes a statement about this topic.

> **Matthew 24:14** And this gospel of the kingdom shall be preached in all the world for a witness unto all nations; and then shall the end come.

This is a ministry on behalf of the world itself, and our preaching demonstration is before the nations. When we take the Kingdom in the manner in which God dictates, this will set the stage for the end. Preaching to the nations is a far different concept than preaching to every creature. When the Kingdom issues are addressed, it will hasten the advent of the end of all things. In the timetable of our Father, this Kingdom business must occur according to plan.

> **Matthew 10:34-38** Think not that I am come to send peace on earth: I came not to send peace, but a sword. 35 For I am come to set a man at variance against his father, and the daughter against her mother, and the daughter in law against her mother in law. 36 And a man's foes shall be they of his own household. 37 He that loveth father or mother more than me is not worthy of me: and he that loveth son or daughter more than me is not worthy of me. 38 And he that taketh not his cross, and followeth after me, is not worthy of me.

Within the body of Christ there is a constant friction between those who follow hard after God and those who are merely in the family. Those who lived a dormant and immature existence exasperated Paul.

> **Hebrews 5:12-13** For when for the time ye ought to be teachers, ye have need that one teach you again which be the first principles of the oracles of God; and are become such as have need of milk, and not of strong meat. 13 For every one that useth milk is unskilful in the word of righteousness: for he is a babe.
>
> **1 Peter 2:2** As newborn babes, desire the sincere milk of the word, that ye may grow thereby:

Milk is for babies, and it is essential for initial development. Yet, there comes a time in the life of each believer to move into a meatier existence.

THE ENTRY PASS

Our Heavenly Father desires for us to be trusted sons and to know Him intimately. Our heart must cry to Him in the language of deep devotion. This is the only way to really know and serve Him in the fullest measure. Only then will we be useful in the highest places of service to Him.

> **Romans 8:15** For ye have not received the spirit of bondage again to fear; but ye have

received the Spirit of adoption, whereby we cry, Abba, Father.

The entry pass is our relationship with the Father. We receive the spirit of adoption which is a transitional authority given when we begin to cry "Abba, Father." We begin to have a burden and a hunger to draw near to the Father and are no longer satisfied with a long distance relationship. We cry with a passion to know Him and begin to seek His heart.

Many believers do not know this place of passionate response to God. Subsequently, they exist as detached children living far below their heritage in God. They may be born again, but the designation of sons and heirs might forever elude them.

Promotion only comes from the Heavenly Father, but it does not come without a personal cost on our part (Psalm 75:6-7). In order to grow in Him, we have to know Him. As we become closer to God, He entrusts us with increasing revelation and responsibility. Those that focus their prayers on knowing and passionately loving their Heavenly Father and pay the price of obedience will continually be promoted, and this is what it means to be an heir and joint-heir with Christ Jesus.

A Word To The Body Of Christ

> **Acts 28:26-27** Saying, Go unto this people, and say, Hearing ye shall hear, and shall not understand; and seeing ye shall see, and not perceive: 27 For the heart of this people is waxed gross, and their ears are dull of hearing, and their eyes have they closed; lest they should see with their eyes, and hear with their ears, and understand with their heart, and should be converted, and I should heal them.

Many will choose not to hear and subsequently will not be converted or healed. This is written to a religious core of individuals. Each of the seven churches of Asia in Revelation is given a stern admonition by Jesus that they must hear if they have ears. This address is to churches, not the unbelievers. The church must begin to hear the call of the Lord and gain His vision.

> **Matthew 13:15-17** For this people's heart is waxed gross, and their ears are dull of hearing, and their eyes they have closed; lest at any time they should see with their eyes, and hear with their ears, and should understand with their heart, and should be converted, and I should heal them. 16 But blessed are your eyes, for they see: and your ears, for they hear. 17 For verily I say unto you, That many prophets and righteous men have desired to see those things which ye see, and have not seen them; and to hear those things which ye hear, and have not heard them.

Jesus declares a blessing for the eyes that will permit perception and a blessing for the ears so they may hear. I declare now that the anointing of the Word of God will come upon you, dear reader. Let your eyes be blessed in order that you might clearly see, your ears touched to hear, and your heart prepared to accept a fresh conversion from your Heavenly Father.

The Saints Of Righteousness

THE POST-RESURRECTION MINISTRY OF THE HOLY GHOST

When Jesus was speaking to His disciples about what would happen after He ascended, He assured them that it was better for them that He go to the Father.

> **John 16:7** Nevertheless I tell you the truth; It is expedient for you that I go away: for if I go not away, the Comforter will not come unto you; but if I depart, I will send him unto you.

How could it be expedient for the disciples that Jesus go away from them? The human mind is incapable of grasping the power and meaning of this statement. How could anything be more beautiful than having Jesus at your side in the natural? Simply put, the only thing that could be better is to join Him and our Heavenly Father in the place of sonship.

The Bible tells us in many ways that Jesus was a first-fruit and a first-born of many brethren. As believers move forward into the deeper things of God, the power to become sons is utilized. Saints are to be the agents of righteousness in this world today. When we view the verse about the expedient nature of Christ's ascension and compare it with the verses which immediately follow, we glean a picture of this ministry of righteousness that is fantastic.

> **John 16:8-14** And when he is come, he will reprove the world of sin, and of righteousness, and of judgment: 9 Of sin, because they believe not on me; 10 Of righteousness, because I go to my Father, and ye see me no more; 11 Of judgment, because the prince of this world is judged. 12 I have yet many things to say unto you, but ye cannot bear them now. 13 Howbeit when he, the Spirit of truth, is come, he will guide you into all truth: for he shall not speak of himself; but whatsoever he shall hear, that shall he speak: and he will shew you things to come. 14 He shall glorify me: for he shall receive of mine, and shall shew it unto you.

The Holy Ghost is sent to glorify Jesus by continuing His mission and pattern in us. He will teach us and lead us in the paths of righteousness for His name's sake. In doing this He will adapt a three-fold ministry that will reprove the world of righteousness, sin and judgment.

Righteousness must be established. The world must be reproved of sin, and the prince of this world must summarily be judged and removed from power.

REPROVING THE WORLD

Righteousness has been fundamentally interpreted as "right standing" with God. Justification is an English word that is randomly translated from the same original as righteousness. Playing off of the English translation we say that justification renders the believer to a position that is "just as if I" had never sinned. These are able depictions of our place in God after being born again. However, righteousness is so much more for the believer. God is the God of righteousness.

The Bible says that:

- His Name is the Lord our Righteousness – Jeremiah 23:6
- He rules with a Sceptre of Righteousness – Hebrews 1:8
- He wears a Breastplate of Righteousness – Isaiah 59:16-17
- He transacts Righteousness in His Wings – Malachi 4:2

The Holy Ghost comes to transact a three-fold ministry in our day. When He reproves the world of righteousness, He is working with the sons of God on earth to restore this world to what God originally intended for it to become. Saints are to be agents of God's plans and purposes. God intended for this planet to be a glorious place of worship and adoration before Him. Satan once served as the director of this worship and did so until his rebellion against God. Subsequently, the planet was decimated by the destruction of rebellion and judgment. When Adam was created God wanted to restore the planet to its original condition, but sin entered, and a curse prevailed. Adam and Eve "missed the mark" of their purpose before the Lord. Instead of believing God, they believed the enemy and disobeyed.

The second Adam, our Lord Jesus Christ, came and restored the privilege of moving in righteousness. When He ascended to the Father, the Holy Ghost was sent to transact the business of restoring the earth to what God intended. When we reprove the world of righteousness and sin, we are saying that God has a purpose for this earth, and we need to realign with that purpose.

In the Greek language the word for **sin** is *hamartia*, which means to miss the mark. Since righteousness has not been the rule of order for the earth, mankind continually misses the mark. In reproving the world of sin and righteousness, we correct misalignment. The Word of God tells us that it is with the heart that man believes unto righteousness, and we wear spiritual armor that includes a breastplate of righteousness.

> **Ephesians 6:14** Stand therefore, having your loins girt about with truth, and having on the breastplate of righteousness;

Paul writes to the Thessalonians that our breastplate is one of faith and love which means that we begin by loving the Father, and we progress to ascertain the marching orders of faith. Righteousness follows suit, and we go forth to transact this vital Kingdom responsibility.

> **1 Thessalonians 5:8** But let us, who are of the day, be sober, putting on the breastplate of faith and love; and for an helmet, the hope of salvation.

THE ESSENCE OF RIGHTEOUSNESS

As we approach the end of all things, it is important that the first man to transact righteousness on behalf of mankind was Abraham. This mighty individual is the father of all who walk in faith, the father of the Jews, and the father of the Arab nations. This is a significant fact to understand as the antichrist will undoubtedly utilize these credentials as a means to acceptance among all three groups.

Abraham enjoyed a peculiar relationship with the Most High, and his pathway of righteousness is detailed within the first book of the Bible. A rather unusual episode in his life is prefaced by a mysterious individual known as the King of Righteousness.

- **Blessed Be Abraham**

After Abraham went forth in battle to rescue Lot from a group of militant warriors, he met a man name Melchizedek who was the King of Salem. The Book of Hebrews identifies this man as also being the King of Righteousness. Truly, both names fit as there will be no righteousness unless it is appropriated through a battle that triumphs in peace.

> **Hebrews 7:2** To whom also Abraham gave a tenth part of all; first being by interpretation King of righteousness, and after that also King of Salem, which is, King of peace;

> **Genesis 14:18-20** And Melchizedek king of Salem brought forth bread and wine: and he was the priest of the most high God. 19 And he blessed him, and said, Blessed be Abram of the most high God, possessor of heaven and earth: 20 And blessed be the most high God, which hath delivered thine enemies into thy hand. And he gave him tithes of all.

Abraham recognized this man as being a representative of the Lord God, and he paid tithes to him. Melchizedek references the connection between heaven and Abraham's earthly victory.

- **Counted For Righteousness**

Shortly after this encounter with the King of Righteousness, Abraham is led forth to a meeting with the Lord. The stars of heaven are linked with Abraham's earthly promise. Abraham is told to speak to the stars about what God has promised upon the earth.

> **Genesis 15:5-6** And he brought him forth abroad, and said, Look now toward heaven, and tell the stars, if thou be able to number them: and he said unto him, So shall thy seed be. 6 And he believed in the LORD; and he counted it to him for righteousness.

Abraham believed God! What magnificent faith, especially since what God told him seemed to have nothing to do with how Abraham's immediate challenge was going to be answered. God had something more in mind than Isaac's birth. God was speaking of the days when righteousness would be trumpeted throughout the earth once again.

Note the connection between the stars of heaven and the promise of righteousness. Stars are associated in the Bible with angels. The angels are mightily associated with Kingdom business and righteousness.

King David speaks of this righteous connection between the earth and heaven.

> **Psalm 85:10-13** Mercy and truth are met together; righteousness and peace have kissed each other. 11 Truth shall spring out of the earth; and righteousness shall look down from heaven. 12 Yea, the LORD shall give that which is good; and our land shall yield her increase. 13

Righteousness shall go before him; and shall set us in the way of his steps.

Righteousness looks down from heaven. Hosea 10:12 tells us that God will rain down righteousness upon us. Additionally, in Isaiah 45:8 God tells the heavens to drop down in order to let the skies pour down righteousness so that righteousness would spring up from the earth. Also, in Psalm 23 David declares that we are led in the paths of righteousness in accordance with the name of God.

- **Lord Of Sabaoth**

The Lord of Sabaoth, or the Lord of Hosts, is the designation wherein God aligns His seed and the angels.

> **Romans 9:29** And as Esaias said before, Except the Lord of **Sabaoth** (Hosts- Isaiah 1:9) had left us a seed, we had been as Sodoma, and been made like unto Gomorrha.
>
> **Galations 3:16-19** Now to Abraham and his seed were the promises made. He saith not, And to seeds, as of many; but as of one, And to thy seed, which is Christ. 17 And this I say, that the covenant, that was confirmed before of God in Christ, the law, which was four hundred and thirty years after, cannot disannul, that it should make the promise of none effect. 18 For if the inheritance be of the law, it is no more of promise: but God gave it to Abraham by promise. 19 Wherefore then serveth the law? It was added because of transgressions, till the seed should come to whom the promise was made; and it was ordained by angels in the hand of a mediator.

The Lord of Hosts, or Lord Sabaoth, is the representation of God as commander of the angelic forces. The **seed** here is the *spermos* of God and embodies His purpose and presence for us and the rest of His creation. For all living things, seed promises reproduction of the forebearer. In essence, these angels are guarding over the original purposes of God when they oversee the seed. Much of God's original intent for the earth is deeply planted as dormant seed waiting for the latter rain to stimulate it into fresh bloom.

Consequently, the seed of God is found within the earth itself. His seed has been planted within the church through Christ Jesus our Lord. The rain of the Spirit will cause each of these plantings to spring to life, and the angels will labor to ensure the harvest that God intends.

There is a closeness between the words "Sabaoth" and "Sabbath." There is no Sabbath without first a full six days of work. Similarly, there is not Sabaoth involvement unless there is a full commitment of man to the task of accomplishing God's ways. Note the partnership between the righteous saints and the angels in instituting the blueprint of God for our world. There is much work to do, and there will be no resting peace until that work is completed.

Jesus taught a parable in Matthew 13:24-39 that speaks of wheat, tares, and the end of the world. The parable is lengthily recounted. Consider with me three verses of the parable.

> **Matthew 13:35, 38-39** That it might be fulfilled which was spoken by the prophet, saying, I will open my mouth in parables; I will utter things which have been kept secret from the foundation of the world. 38 The field is the world; the good seed are the children of the kingdom; but the tares are the children of the wicked one; 39 The enemy that sowed them is the devil; the harvest is the end of the world; and the reapers are the angels.

From the foundation of the world, God's seed has been planted within His creation. The enemy attempted to corrupt the purposes of the Lord by virtue of the planting of unrighteous seed. As the end of the world is nearing, both of these harvests are growing simultaneously. The saints will partner with the angels of the Lord in the separating of these two factions. Righteousness will prevail.

The Holy Ghost has come in order to reprove the world of sin and righteousness. He has also come to empower the church to do battle with the prince of this world. According to Isaiah 4:4-5, judgment paves the way for the glory of God.

JUDGING THE PRINCE OF THIS WORLD

Currently, there is a well-organized and integrated system of demonic control over much of the planet. Reports that the enemy has no power are premature. The command that Jesus gave in John 16 concerning the coming of the Comforter references a time after the cross and resurrection, remaining a valid mandate for today. The prince of this world is not Satan himself, but a controlling potentate that regulates the demonic system. The Apostle Paul says some amazing things about this evil ruler.

> **2 Corinthians 4:3-4** But if our gospel be hid, it is hid to them that are lost: 4 In whom the god of this world hath blinded the minds of them which believe not, lest the light of the glorious gospel of Christ, who is the image of God, should shine unto them.

While Jesus depicted this being as the prince of this world, the Apostle Paul addresses this individual as the god of this world. Jesus addressed the matter as it really was in the spirit realm, as this is a fallen principality. Paul spoke from the vantage point of the prideful perception within the world system and demonic realm. This evil ruler is currently in control of major portions of this globe while receiving little or no opposition from the general church. Part of his strength lies in the contention by the church that he does not exist.

The world is currently enslaved by this force of darkness. The Scripture tells us that there is only one measure of relief. The light of truth must be properly directed into the darkness. The falsehood of enemy rule must be debunked, and the saints must be led into these regions through intercession and prophetic pursuit. Jesus spoke of the reality of this conflict.

> **Matthew 11:12** And from the days of John the Baptist until now the kingdom of heaven suffereth violence, and the violent take it by force.

Violence is an occupation by force, and the only way to eradicate it is by confronting it with a greater force of violence. The New Testament instructs that taking strongholds and waging a good warfare is the responsibility of the church. This is not a political show of opinion or a token protest. It is warfare, and there is no convenient way to conduct or describe it.

STRONGHOLDS

> **Luke 11:21-22** When a strong man armed keepeth his palace, his goods are in peace: 22 But when a stronger than he shall come upon him, and overcome him, he taketh from him all his armour wherein he trusted, and divideth his spoils.

Jesus established the fact that there are strongholds that are occupied by strongmen who have armor and spoils. When a "stronger than he" comes upon the palace, the land and people are delivered. This is a mission that is precisely ordained of the Most High and not random or rogue in any sense. God directs the saints and empowers them to overcome strongholds of His choosing. From the deposed strongman the saint takes the armor wherein the enemy trusts. This is a depiction of the anointing and original purpose of the terrain.

Places have anointing and purpose according to the blueprint of the original creation of this world. The enemy utilizes initial intent and anointing in order to create climates of unusual spiritual activity. This is why certain places on the map are infamous for particular sinful behaviors.

Within this atmosphere the enemy entices those who will worship and serve him either through music, debauchery or some other addictive device. When the saint welcomes the calling of God and begins to partner with Him through prayer to come against these strongholds, people will be freed from the blinding influences that were being enforced by the defeated foe. Places can be turned from centers of evil into places of devoted worship to the Lord God. The goods that were possessed by the enemy are spoiled as people are freed to worship God and declare the song of the redeemed. There is no love like that which flows from one who has been forgiven much. God promises that the treasures of darkness will be given to His anointed ones.

> **Isaiah 45:3** And I will give thee the *treasures of darkness*, and hidden riches of secret places, that thou mayest know that I, the Lord, which call thee by thy name, am the God of Israel.

This depiction is a defining of people and places. God wants to redeem the world, and that includes all of His creation. The greatest treasure of darkness is the redeemed individual that turns from the bondage of evil into the freedom of God.

This is global evangelism in its highest form. This is why the saint must ascertain what God is requiring and go where He sends. He who controls the harvest field controls the harvest. God is looking for mighty men to contend for fields of operation. Although a more detailed discussion of this and other warfare topics is found in the book entitled **Princes**, for this study we must take a closer look at how righteousness is opposed on the earth.

ENEMIES OF RIGHTEOUSNESS

The Word of God lists two major enemies of righteousness: religion and demonic operatives. Let us first consider the realm of religious opposition.

- **Opposition From The Religious Spirit**

2 Corinthians 3:7-9 But if the ministration of death, written and engraven in stones, was glorious, so that the children of Israel could not stedfastly behold the face of Moses for the glory of his countenance; which glory was to be done away: 8 How shall not the ministration of the spirit be rather glorious? 9 For if the ministration of condemnation be glory, much more doth the ministration of righteousness exceed in glory.

The law that was replaced by grace is a type depicting the fact that any new move of God will be resisted by the constriction of the last wineskin. Religion is an enemy of righteousness in that it typically resists new progression and acquisition.

God calls the basis of the law a "ministration of condemnation." Although it is clear that there was a glory attached to this ministration, condemnation occurs whenever the new demonstration of grace arrives. We must guard against the errant position of withstanding the newest flow of the Spirit of God. For if we resist the flow of righteousness, we become an enemy of righteousness.

- **Opposition From Demonic Spirits**

The second enemy of righteousness that the saint will face is that of advanced demonic structure. This system is based in the heavenlies and is highly developed on the earth.

Matthew 24:24 For there shall arise false Christs, and false prophets, and shall shew great signs and wonders; insomuch that, if it were possible, they shall deceive the very elect.

2 Corinthians 11:13-15   For such are false apostles, deceitful workers, transforming themselves into the apostles of Christ. 14 And no marvel; for Satan himself is transformed into an angel of light. 15 Therefore it is no great thing if his ministers also be transformed as the ministers of righteousness; whose end shall be according to their works.

The enemy develops avid followers for his own purposes. Active recruitment for the kingdom of darkness is currently being demonstrated throughout the earth. While the connective between God and His saints is love, the connection within the enemy camp consists of manifold variations of perverted passions and earthly power.

THE EXAMPLE OF TYRE

An Old Testament example of this demonic structure between Satan and an earth-based enemy of righteousness is found in Ezekiel 28 and involves two characters referred to as the prince of Tyre and the king of Tyre.

Ezekiel 28:2-7   Son of man, say unto the prince of Tyrus, Thus saith the Lord God; Because thine heart is lifted up, and thou hast said, I am a God, I sit in the seat of God, in the midst of the seas; yet thou art a man, and not God, though thou set thine heart as the heart of God: 3 Behold, thou art wiser than Daniel; there is no secret that they can hide from thee: 4 With thy wisdom and with thine understanding thou hast gotten thee riches, and hast gotten gold and silver into thy treasures: 5 By thy great wisdom and by thy traffick hast thou increased thy riches, and thine heart is lifted up because of thy riches: 6 Therefore thus saith the Lord God; Because thou hast set thine heart as the heart of God; 7 Behold, therefore I will bring strangers upon thee, the terrible of the nations: and they shall draw their swords against the beauty of thy wisdom, and they shall defile thy brightness.

This passage speaks of a man who considers himself to be a god. He possesses wealth, power, and supernatural insight of a kind likened to that of Daniel. This man, classified as the prince of Tyre, has affiliated himself with the devil. While the man is regarded as a prince, the devil is classified as the king of the area.

Ezekiel 28:12-16 Son of man, take up a lamentation upon the king of Tyrus, and say unto him, Thus saith the Lord God; Thou sealest up the sum, full of wisdom, and perfect in beauty. 13 Thou hast been in Eden the garden of God; every precious stone was thy covering, the sardius, topaz, and the diamond, the beryl, the onyx, and the jasper, the sapphire, the emerald, and the carbuncle, and gold: the workmanship of thy tabrets and of thy pipes was prepared in thee in the day that thou wast created. 14 Thou art the anointed cherub that covereth; and I have set thee so: thou wast upon the holy mountain of God; thou hast walked up and down in the midst of the stones of fire. 15 Thou wast perfect in thy ways from the day that thou wast created, till iniquity was found in thee. 16 By the multitude of thy merchandise they have filled the midst of thee with violence, and thou hast sinned: therefore I will cast thee as profane out of the mountain of God: and I will destroy thee, O covering cherub, from the midst of the stones of fire.

This depiction is universally regarded as one of the devil himself. Classified as the king of Tyre he is undoubtedly the one who empowers the earthly prince of Tyre. This type of partnership is not isolated to the Old Testament. There are some New Testament examples of demonic enemies of righteousness.

ELYMAS

Acts 13:8-10 But Elymas the sorcerer (for so is his name by interpretation) **withstood** them, seeking to turn away the deputy from the faith. 9 Then Saul, (who also is called Paul,) filled with the Holy Ghost, set his eyes on him, 10 And said, O full of all subtilty and all mischief, thou child of the devil, thou enemy of all righteousness, wilt thou not cease to pervert the right ways of the Lord

Here is the personification of the stronghold concept. Paul classifies this sorcerer as being a child of the devil and an enemy of all righteousness. Elymas dominated the spirit realm within the entire city and region. When Paul came onto the scene, Verse 8 states that this sorcerer **withstood** him. A careful examination of the Greek word utilized for **withstood** reveals vital insights in the arena of spiritual warfare. The word *anthisthema* means to stand against by virtue of a *histhemi*, or established power base. God wants us to evict the enemy from power bases so that we can establish the power base of righteousness.

Histhemi is utilized by Jesus to depict strongholds in which the enemy dwells on earth. Of the many examples, perhaps the most demonstrative is that which is found in the Gospel of Luke.

> **Luke 11:18** If Satan also be divided against himself, how shall his kingdom **stand**?

We utilize *histhemi* in our vernacular to speak of allergens that populate the areas of a country. Whenever a person who has an allergy enters this region where the histamine is prevalent, there is a physical reaction. In the context of spiritual warfare, when we apostolically enter a territory we will encounter the *histhemi* of that area. The ruling force will withstand us by virtue of its particular weaponry just as Elymas **withstood** (*anthisthema*) Paul and his comrades.

Paul was also withstood in similar fashion by Alexander the coppersmith, an agent of a principality known as Diana. This man was an enemy of righteousness that Paul subsequently warred against in true spiritual fashion. When embarking upon the spiritual quest that led him into the region, the Apostle speaks of what came against him, both physically and spiritually.

> **2 Corinthians 7:5** For, when we were come into Macedonia, our flesh had no rest, but we were troubled on every side; without were fightings, within were fears

There will be those of the enemy kingdom that will partner with rulers of darkness. These men and women will also stand against the apostles who are sent into the realm with the gospel of the Kingdom. Listen to what Paul says about Alexander and Hymenaeus.

> **2 Timothy 4:14-15** Alexander the coppersmith did me much evil: the Lord reward him according to his works: 15 Of whom be thou ware also; for he hath greatly *withstood* our words.

> **1 Timothy 1:20** Of whom is Hymenaeus and Alexander; whom I have delivered unto Satan, that they may learn not to blaspheme.

While many believers may have been tempted to surrender someone to the devil in this manner, before you enter into this realm of warfare, make certain that you are operating against an enemy of righteousness and that God has directed you to do so. Otherwise, you may become just as vile as the force that opposes you.

Paul writes to Timothy that Moses also was withstood by enemies of righteousness. When God sent him to the court of Pharaoh, the magicians of Pharaoh's court were a frontline defense for the enemy.

> **2 Timothy 3:8** Now as Jannes and Jambres *withstood* Moses...

These two individuals were obviously based in Egypt as the earthly representatives of darkness. Subsequently Moses utilized the power of God to defeat the powers of darkness. Greater is He that is within us than he that is in the world (1 John 4:4).

For the saint, the concepts of withstanding and standing are operative words of conquest and establishment. This is ably demonstrated in Paul's discussion of the armor of God.

> **Ephesians 6:13** Wherefore take unto you the whole armour of God, that ye may be able to withstand in the evil day, and having done all, to stand.

Quite simply, we drive the enemy out and establish a stand for the Lord. Our principle offensive weapon in Ephesians is a verbal one characterized as the sword of the Spirit, the Word of God. Jesus defines this further in Luke's Gospel.

> **Luke 21:15** For I will give you a mouth and wisdom, which all your adversaries shall not be able to gainsay nor resist.

God's *rhema* word will provide wisdom as well as declaration that the enemy will not be able to **resist** *(anthisthema)*. What an incredible promise! Whenever we resist the devil in this way, he will not be able to withstand us, and he will flee.

> **James 4:7** Submit yourselves therefore to God. **Resist** the devil, and he will flee from you.

As we submit ourselves to God, He places us in the position that we must inhabit for righteousness' sake. As we devotedly fulfill this task, God will grant to us the insights and power to resist the *histhemi* of the enemy.

In comparing the past two passages, we find that in Luke 21 the enemy cannot stand against the wisdom of God that comes forth from our mouths. Within this passage in James, we are told that as we submit to God, we will be able to withstand the attacks of the enemy that would try to uproot us. In fact, the Greek word that describes his fleeing is the word *phuego*. Phonetically, this word has evolved into the word for fire in some modern languages. Hence, when we submit ourselves to God and declare what He is saying through us, we are resisting in a way that causes the devil to flee for his life like someone fleeing a fire.

The Apostle Paul also faced other people that were operatives of the enemy kingdom. Although they are not specifically labeled as enemies of righteousness, they follow the pattern of what we perceived regarding Elymas, Alexander and Jannes/Jambres.

SIMON

> **Acts 8:9-11** But there was a certain man, called Simon, which beforetime in the same city used sorcery, and bewitched the people of Samaria, giving out that himself was some great one: 10 To whom they all gave heed, from the least to the greatest, saying, This man is the great power of God. 11 And to him they had regard, because that of long time he had bewitched them with sorceries.

Simon had a reputation that labeled him the "great power of god." This is quite a pretentious title, and it typifies the kind of demonic structuring currently found on earth. He had established a seat of power in the region, and he desired to keep it. As opposed to Elymas, Simon elected to join what he could not defeat.

In Simon-like fashion, enemies of righteousness will undoubtedly elect to attempt to join with the triumphant forces of God. In a similar manner, the Gibeonites were permitted to join the ranks of the children of Israel during the rule of Joshua. Israel regretted that foolish decision from that day forward. In this day, we must remain vigilant in order to prevent the enemy from infiltrating our camp as we advance in the process of kingdom taking.

PUTHOS OF MACEDONIA

> **Acts 16:9** And a vision appeared to Paul in the night; There **stood** a man of Macedonia, and prayed him, saying, Come over into Macedonia, and help us

Paul and his comrades were compelled by an angelic night vision to redirect their stated course in order to take the gospel into Macedonia. Interestingly, the angel that appeared to Paul in the night was operating in a *histhemi* of God's choosing. When this heavenly representative stood, he was functioning in a *histhemi* of God's original claim to the earth. Undoubtedly, this angelic visitor was assigned to partner with Paul and the intercessors that were at that very moment encamped in prayer beside a river in Macedonia.

When Paul and his entourage arrived in the region, they met a group of women that were praying at the riverside. Their "stand" in prayer was efficacious in mobilizing the angel of the Lord, which then proceeded from that intercessory stand to visit Paul in the night. Other spiritual forces in the region were also maneuvering.

> **Acts 16:16** And it came to pass, as we went to prayer, a certain damsel possessed with a spirit

of divination met us, which brought her masters much gain by soothsaying:

The spirit of divination was evidently a controlling influence in the Philippian community. There was an infrastructure in place for a spirit to speak prophetically through a young girl to an entire city, and Paul summarily went head to head with this spirit. Interestingly, the apostle waited a number of days before affecting this warfare maneuver implying that he waited on the Lord for the word of direction and timing. These are essential elements to any successful warfare.

LESSONS FOR TODAY

Look at your city. Are there areas that are known for certain types of debauchery and evil? Throughout the decades do these areas remain the same in portraying certain types of sin and darkness? These regions quite probably are under the current control of enemies of righteousness. The evil in recurrent demonstration is undoubtedly a ***histhemi,*** which pollutes generation after generation. Intercession is the key to knowing what God would have you to do and not do in respect to these areas of darkness.

Spiritual warfare will not be successful unless absolutely directed and empowered by God. The saints are not a band of willful soldiers of fortune that go forth on random crusades. God is training His people to overcome the structures of the enemy. We must be servants of the Greater One, and we must be absolutely devoted to His timing.

The King Of Saints

INTERCESSION OF THE SAINTS

The saints are going to battle against the enemies of God in the last days! Regardless of your particular viewpoint regarding the eschatological timeline, it is hard to argue with the fact that the Bible declares a vital role for the saints.

You remember Enoch, do you not? For the seventh from Adam, fellowship with the Father was a life pursuit.

> **Genesis 5:24** And Enoch walked with God: and he was not; for God took him.

No wonder God allowed Enoch to prophesy concerning the mobilization of a mighty army of saints. A similar calling of devotion and fellowship will be the watchwords for the lifestyle of the saints.

> **Jude 14** And Enoch also, the seventh from Adam, prophesied of these, saying, Behold, the Lord cometh with ten thousands of his saints.

Moses, the great lawgiver and friend of God, also spoke of the saints as being ten thousand in number within the hand of the Lord.

> **Deuteronomy 33:1-3** And this is the blessing, wherewith Moses the man of God blessed the children of Israel before his death. 2 And he said, The Lord came from Sinai, and rose up from Seir unto them; he shined forth from mount Paran,

> and he came with ten thousands of saints: from his right hand went a fiery law for them. 3 Yea, he loved the people; all his saints are in thy hand: and they sat down at thy feet; every one shall receive of thy words.

These saints sit at the feet of God and receive His words of life. Suffice it to say that God has continually loved this special group of people. They are His choice servants and friends, and they treat Him with utmost closeness and devotion.

Our conquering Lord is coming with a host of saints, and they will war at His side against the forces of Satan. What will keep them fueled and ready for the conflict is continual fellowship with the Heavenly Father. We must be a praying people, and we must do it without ceasing, utilizing every mode of prayer before God. In many ways we will need to become modern day Enochs. The thought of not being a prayer warrior is both unheard of and impractical.

HARPS AND VIALS

In the book of Revelation we behold many significant insights that connect the saints with the events of heaven. One thing that is continually depicted is that the saints are a worshipping and praying people. While this topic is more notably covered in the companion volume, **Pneumatikos**, look at the description of the elders and angels in Revelation Chapter 8.

> **Revelation 8:3** And another angel came and stood at the altar, having a golden censer; and there was given unto him much incense, that he should offer it with the prayers of all saints upon the golden altar which was before the throne.

The prayers of the saints carry immense merit before the Heavenly Father. These prayers will be released in incredibly powerful fashion in the heavens. The angelic host will treat these intercessions with great care and reverence.

> **Revelation 5:8** And when he had taken the book, the four beasts and four and twenty elders fell down before the Lamb, having every one of them harps, and golden vials full of odours, which are the prayers of saints.

These saintly prayers have vitality as God visits the earth with fiery judgments in direct response to the cry of His people. The words of the saints before the Father will be crucial in the climactic events that are portrayed in the final book of the Bible.

PRAYER RELEASES JUDGMENTS

> **Revelation 8:1, 3-5** And when he had opened the seventh seal, there was silence in heaven about the space of half an hour. 3 And another angel came and stood at the altar, having a golden censer; and there was given unto him

> much incense, that he should offer it with the prayers of all saints upon the golden altar which was before the throne. 4 And the smoke of the incense, which came with the prayers of the saints, ascended up before God out of the angel's hand. 5 And the angel took the censer, and filled it with fire of the altar, and cast it into the earth: and there were voices, and thunderings, and lightnings, and an earthquake

Here is another powerful example of the efficacy of the intercession of the saints. Note the progression found within Verse 5: Voices of intercession and worship before the Father are the impetus of a powerful set of occurrences. Thunderings quickly follow the voices, and this represents a changing climate and atmosphere. Quite literally, the hand of God is moved by the voices and there is an immediate transformation. Thunder represents a clashing of influences, and this is an impressive picture of the violent taking the kingdom by force.

Lightning is a depictive of quick and decisive transacting of the purpose of the Lord. Whether the casting down of Satan, or a bolt of vengeance from the hand of God upon some stronghold of injustice, lightning is a suddenly of God's applied judgment. Earthquakes typify the result of these changes upon the earth.

God tells us that there is silence in heaven for thirty minutes. Theories abound as to the meaning of this suspension of sound.

Could it be that God is telling us that the sounds of heaven that have governed creation are now allowing the sounds of the saints from earth to hold sway?

What is the meaning of the thirty-minute time sequence? The Bible tells us that a day in the Lord is as a thousand years. If we apply that measuring device to thirty minutes, we deduce a period of roughly forty years on earth. This is the generation of the saints. While we cannot say when it began, we are sure that we exist within that time frame right now. These are exciting days to be alive in the Lord.

WARFARE

Battle of a sort that has not been known on this globe is described in the book of Daniel, and it involves the saints of the Lord. While it is not the scope of this book to attempt an interpretation of the time that these events will happen, it is important that we understand some of the responsibilities of the saints.

> **Daniel 7:21-25** I beheld, and the same horn made war with the saints, and prevailed against them; 22 Until the Ancient of days came, and judgment was given to the saints of the most High; and the time came that the saints possessed the kingdom. 23 Thus he said, The fourth beast shall be the fourth kingdom upon

earth, which shall be diverse from all kingdoms, and shall devour the whole earth, and shall tread it down, and break it in pieces. 24 And the ten horns out of this kingdom are ten kings that shall arise: and another shall rise after them; and he shall be diverse from the first, and he shall subdue three kings. 25 And he shall speak great words against the most High, and shall wear out the saints of the most High, and think to change times and laws: and they shall be given into his hand until a time and times and the dividing of time.

Revelation 13:7 And it was given unto him to make war with the saints, and to overcome them: and power was given him over all kindreds, and tongues, and nations.

There will be an ongoing struggle on the planet for the fulfillment of the purpose of the Father. God will allow the saints to be mightily triumphant at times, but He will also allow them to be temporarily overcome. Note from the previously cited passages that the enemy will attempt to "wear out" the saints of the Most High. Faithfulness is a vital component to the end-time church. Jesus spoke of this in the Book of Matthew.

Matthew 25:21 His lord said unto him, Well done, thou good and faithful servant: thou hast been faithful over a few things, I will make thee ruler over many things: enter thou into the joy of thy lord.

As previously discussed in Chapter 8, for the saint of the end times, being called and chosen is not enough. There must also be faithfulness to duty and commissioning. The Apostle Paul spoke of how the first sign of the apostolic is patience. Patience implies a devotion to duty and an understanding of your mission. Impatience is often the result of selfishness or a lack of appreciation for the challenges involved in the task itself. Remember that the saint is an end-time prophet, and that designation was ordained from the foundation of the world.

> **Luke 11:50** That the blood of all the prophets, which was shed from the foundation of the world, may be required of this generation;

The faith of the saints is simply defined as that which commits to the purpose and plan of the Heavenly Father as the saint is committed to His eternal service. We are aligned with Christ and are to be fully devoted to the plan of God – no matter the cost. Let us further consider the patience of the saints.

> **Revelation 13:10** He that leadeth into captivity shall go into captivity: he that killeth with the sword must be killed with the sword. Here is the patience and the faith of the saints.

> **Revelation 14:12** Here is the patience of the saints: here are they that keep the commandments of God, and the faith of Jesus.

We cannot help but notice that the saint is mightily possessed by a spirit of patience and faithfulness. While we are motivated by *agape*, the manner in which we protect ourselves in the conflicts of the spirit realm is through faith. Faith is our shield, and we must not allow anything to corrupt our protective covering.

Within Christendom, it has been said that faith is a leap. For the saint, faith is a patient suspension in midair as we wait for the fullness of the Father. Faith is calling things that be not as though they are already in existence. The saint will speak these things and stand in seemingly impossible places of faith. This is righteousness in its fullest measure.

CROSS OF THE SAINTS

In Revelation there are many graphic depictions of the sacrifices that the saints will offer in their obedience to the commands of the Father. Here are a few examples:

> **Revelation 16:6** For they have shed the blood of saints and prophets, and thou hast given them blood to drink; for they are worthy.

> **Revelation 17:6** And I saw the woman drunken with the blood of the saints, and with the blood of the martyrs of Jesus: and when I saw her, I wondered with great admiration.

Revelation 18:24 And in her was found the blood of prophets, and of saints, and of all that were slain upon the earth.

Not a pretty picture, to say the least. No wonder patience is of such a necessity. No wonder those who are in this company of believers will have to be captivated by love for God. No wonder then that the greatest gift of all is the *agape* of the Heavenly Father. Imagine the power of this saintly group of believers. Grasp the picture of the power of God that will be known by them. Picture the radiant face of the martyred Stephen magnified by thousands. Envision the welcoming arms of a vengeful God as He receives His champions to their eternal home.

14

The Fine Linen Of The Saints

Whenever the Bible utilizes a pattern or a theme, it has great meaning. One such type of meaning is found regarding the Biblical identification of the clothing of the saints. Sometimes the revelation of the meaning is immediately clear, and other times it is progressively understood. This is the case when considering the garments, or fine linen, of the saints.

> **Revelation 19:8** And to her was granted that she should be arrayed in fine linen, clean and white: for the fine linen is the righteousness of saints.

What does it mean to be clad in fine linen that is clean and white? In order to grasp the implied and real meaning of this designation, we must investigate the myriad aspects of the usage of fine linen throughout the Word of God.

COMMITTED TO THE PURPOSE AND PLAN OF GOD

There is no greater example of dedication and commitment to the purpose and plan of God than that which is found in our Lord and Savior, Jesus Christ. Peter calls Him the "Holy One and the Just" in Acts 3:14, which says that He was anointed to do the Father's bidding, and He committed Himself totally toward that end. Paul details this sacred dedication to duty for us in his first epistle to Timothy.

1 Timothy 3:16 And without controversy great is the mystery of godliness: God was manifest in the flesh, justified in the Spirit, seen of angels, preached unto the Gentiles, believed on in the world, received up into glory.

Our Lord established an embodiment of the saintly call. He came to earth to display the mystery of God through the power of the Spirit of the Lord. Righteous deeds were transacted in the presence of the angels and in the presence of the world to which He was sent. As this process culminated in belief of the message, the glory of the Lord touched earth and received Jesus into heaven.

Jesus came into this world and was immediately wrapped in swaddling linen signifying that his life was bound for the purposes of the Father from His birth. The clothing of the Lord after the resurrection is a subtle yet vibrant depiction of our calling to similar devotion. The fact that the linen clothing is folded neatly shows the fullness of the completion of the saintly mission.

John 20:6-7 Then cometh Simon Peter following him, and went into the sepulchre, and seeth the linen clothes lie, 7 And the napkin, that was about his head, not lying with the linen clothes, but wrapped together in a place by itself

Also, the fact that the napkin that was about His head was wrapped in a separate place signifies that each saint must be individually called of the Lord to the task envisioned for them.

While the demonstration of the overall mission of the saints will display similar patterns of obedience and service, the individual calling and purpose is reserved as separate for each one.

WORSHIP LEADERS IN THE TABERNACLE OF DAVID

A saint is a passionate worshipper of God. Amos 9:11 informs us that the tabernacle of David will be re-established in the time of the end. Let us look at what David's seers and tabernacle leaders wore.

> **2 Chronicles 5:12** Also the Levites which were the singers, all of them of Asaph, of Heman, of Jeduthun, with their sons and their brethren, being arrayed in white linen, having cymbals and psalteries and harps, stood at the east end of the altar, and with them an hundred and twenty priests sounding with trumpets:

The principal leaders of Davidic worship were Asaph, Heman, and Jeduthun. The Bible records that each of these men were seers and were uniformly arrayed in fine linen, which is representative of the saints. These men were prophetic worshippers that followed the leading of the king. They were devoted to God, but they also knew how to lead and to be led. All true saints of the Lord will be devoted, prophetic worshippers. They will worship in unrestrained fashion with the fire of the Lord blazing within them.

Perhaps this white linen is the garment of praise of which Isaiah 61:3 speaks, for within that same verse we find a reference to trees of righteousness.

2 Chronicles 5:12 further states that the worship leaders stood at the east end of the altar. This is significant because in the Book of Ezekiel the glory of God is said to reside in the east. The 120 trumpets remind us of the Day of Pentecost when the remnant of 120 waited expectantly for the promise of the Father. This is a picture of those that are clothed with the purpose of worshipping God, welcoming Him in His Glory in accordance with His promise and purpose.

Worship is an integral part of all things within the spirit realm. Worship is a heartfelt devotion and expression that is offered in many ways. Musical offerings are one facet of this devotion, but the strains of true worship can be heard through many modes of fond expression. The enemy knows the full power of worship, since one of his duties before the rebellion in the heavens included the leading of worship before the Father. In this hour, he attempts to employ this principle of power within his own kingdom, and he withstands the development of worship within the church.

Recounting the things that God has done is not that much of a challenge for the enemy. He is already aware of those things.

Worship is creative. If the saints worship God, new things will happen that will disrupt and dispossess the enemy from significant portions of the known world.

Today is a new day. When God's people worship Him, there are creative measures that cannot be predicted or controlled. They will determine the triumph of the hour and of the future. The enemy merely tolerates the recounting of past losses as a necessary annoyance.

Praise is very important. It should be used to inspire the people to believe for the unchanging power of God to visit afresh in this hour. Sadly, most praise is a convenient placebo for the general church. It makes the church feel like they are doing something grand, but it does not really cost them anything. It triumphs something that another group of people experienced. Praise is powerful when it glorifies God and engenders a belief that He is moving today. This leads us into the places of worship before our mighty God and King.

PRIESTLY MINISTRY UNTO GOD

In the Old Testament priests of the Lord were clothed in linen. Saints are called to this ministry of priestly devotion in worship and service before the Lord. Peter classifies the chosen generation and holy/saintly nation as those that are royal priests unto God. When you are said to be a royal priesthood, you are qualified as people that have kingly authority and who minister on behalf of, and to, the King. Herein is a difference between earthly priests and royal priests. The priests of the Old Covenant were those that represented people before God. Royal priests represent God before the earth. They also represent the territories to which they have been assigned before the courts of the God of the universe.

> **1 Peter 2:9** But ye are a chosen generation, a royal priesthood, an holy nation, a peculiar people; that ye should shew forth the praises of him who hath called you out of darkness into his marvellous light:

Ezekiel speaks in mysterious terms of men that serve God in this manner. Both he and Daniel were servants in the courts of heaven and regularly ministered on behalf of God's purpose for the earth. In this ministry they labored beside the angels in bizarre and powerful ways. One of the blessings of the saintly walk is the close relationship that exists between angels and humans that are engaged in the Father's business.

Consider three points of royal ministry that are recorded by a linen-clad saint in Ezekiel's vision.

- **Intercession, Judgment And Protection**

    Ezekiel 9:2-4, 11 And, behold, six men came from the way of the higher gate, which lieth toward the north, and every man a slaughter weapon in his hand; and one man among them was clothed with linen, with a writer's inkhorn by his side: and they went in, and stood beside the brasen altar. 3 And the glory of the God of Israel was gone up from the cherub, whereupon he was, to the threshold of the house. And he called to the man clothed with linen, which had the writer's inkhorn by his side; 4 And the Lord said unto him, Go through the midst of the city, through the midst of Jerusalem, and set a mark upon the foreheads of the men that sigh and that cry for all the abominations that be done in the midst thereof. 11 And, behold, the man clothed with linen, which had the inkhorn by his side, reported the matter, saying, I have done as thou hast commanded me.

We see in this stunning account one man who is clothed in linen accompanying a group of individuals that are armed for war. In Verse 4 this representative of the saints is commanded to mark those who have shared in an intercessory burden for the people of God so that they would not be consumed by God's judgment. This man had an inkhorn indicating that he was responsible for recording and expressing information of importance. This is a saintly ministry.

- **Declaration Against A City**

> **Ezekiel 10:2** And he spake unto the man clothed with linen, and said, Go in between the wheels, even under the cherub, and fill thine hand with coals of fire from between the cherubims, and scatter them over the city. And he went in my sight.

God commands this representative of the royal priesthood to receive coals from the holy altar to be scattered over the city. The saints will represent God in pronouncing judgment over cities, regions, and nations. This is never to be a discretionary pursuit. The Lord himself will command and empower this grave business. The days that are coming upon our planet will precipitate this type of ministry unto the Lord. The saints will employ this tactic over and over again across the globe while battling a sinful world that has pledged themselves to the powers of darkness.

- **Guardians Of God's Glory**

> **Ezekiel 10:6-8** And it came to pass, that when he had commanded the man clothed with linen, saying, Take fire from between the wheels, from between the cherubims; then he went in, and stood beside the wheels. 7 And one cherub stretched forth his hand from between the cherubims unto the fire that was between the cherubims, and took thereof, and put it into the hands of him that was clothed with linen: who took it, and went out. 8 And there appeared in the cherubims the form of a man's hand under their wings.

Upon reading this passage one might ask the question as to what this saint was to do with the fire that was taken from between the cherubim because no mention is made regarding what became of the man or the fire. An explanation is found in the following text where the glory of the Lord departed to the mountains of the east. The saintly man became the representative vessel of God's glory in the city.

When the general church is removed from this planet, the age of the church will basically have concluded. The Holy Ghost who has prevented the antichrist from blossoming prematurely will be removed from that mode of operation on this planet for a time. At that moment the fire of the Lord will be known upon and within the saints in a manner that God has been preparing His people to receive. What an exciting promise!

INTERACTION AND IDENTIFICATION WITH ANGELS

Daniel was a prototype of the modern day saint. In that respect he interacted with the angelic and with saints who were ministering in heaven.

> **Daniel 10:5** Then I lifted up mine eyes, and looked, and behold a certain man clothed in linen, whose loins were girded with fine gold of Uphaz:

The clothing of the angel is remarkable as he was adorned in fine linen which is reserved for the saints. He was sent to Daniel whose intercession and devotion to the Lord caused him to be highly effective in ministry on behalf of the restoration of the nation of Israel. Today, the saints are called to be highly effective on behalf of the restoration of the earth. Let us consider some ways angels interact with their saintly co-workers.

- **Information And Communication Of Timing**

As is the case with the preceding verse, angels are often sent to communicate. Hence, they are literally "messengers." The angel in Daniel 10:5 has a golden belt which represents purest truth depicting that his actions were based on behalf of the highest priority of heaven. The saints interact with these angels and receive important insights and instructions from them.

> **Daniel 8:13** Then I heard one saint speaking, and another saint said unto that certain saint which spake, How long shall be the vision concerning the daily sacrifice, and the transgression of desolation, to give both the sanctuary and the host to be trodden under foot?

Apparently Daniel was interacting with saints in heaven who transacted the business of intercession within the heavens. Note that one inquired of another, and information was exchanged.

Consider a similar query regarding the timing of the Lord by another grouping of linen-clad individuals.

> **Daniel 12:6-7** And one said to the man clothed in linen, which was upon the waters of the river, How long shall it be to the end of these wonders? 7 And I heard the man clothed in linen, which was upon the waters of the river, when he held up his right hand and his left hand unto heaven, and sware by him that liveth for ever that it shall be for a time, times, and an half; and when he shall have accomplished to scatter the power of the holy people, all these things shall be finished.

Wherever inquiring is present in the scriptures between those clothed in linen, some manner of intercession, revelation and declaration of the saints is transpiring. John had a similar encounter in the book of Revelation when he thought he had encountered God.

> **Revelation 22:9** Then saith he unto me, See thou do it not: for I am thy fellowservant, and of thy brethren the prophets, and of them which keep the sayings of this book: worship God.

- **Directing The Saints**

A vital time for the Church was the moment that immediately followed the ascension of the Lord Jesus. There was a saintly call and command for the disciples to go to Jerusalem. Before the men could deliberate or degenerate into inactivity, two messengers in white apparel reminded them of the words of Jesus.

Acts 1:10-11 And while they looked stedfastly toward heaven as he went up, behold, two men stood by them in white apparel; 11 Which also said, Ye men of Galilee, why stand ye gazing up into heaven? this same Jesus, which is taken up from you into heaven, shall so come in like manner as ye have seen him go into heaven.

We often entertain angels unaware in our current life, but we are entering a time when the saints will regularly interact with angels of the Lord who are committed to the saintly function of fulfilling righteousness.

- **Answering The Cry Of Saintly Intercession**

In accordance with what we witness in Revelation 8 regarding the intercession of the saints, we see once again the grouping of seven angels coming forth from the Tabernacle of the Testimony in heaven. This place is open to the saints now, and much of what transpires through intercession occurs here.

These angels are engaged in saintly ministry as they bring forth plagues for the purpose of visiting them upon the earth. These vials are filled with the wrath of God, and that wrath is undoubtedly because of the dastardly warfare that is being carried on against His saints as they conduct the business of God.

Revelation 15:5-6 And after that I looked, and, behold, the temple of the tabernacle of the testimony in heaven was opened: 6 And the seven angels came out of the temple, having the seven plagues, clothed in pure and white linen, and having their breasts girded with golden girdles.

- **Future War**

Enoch prophesied of the Lord coming with an army of saints. This is depicted with great clarity.

> **Revelation 19:14** And the armies which were in heaven followed him upon white horses, clothed in fine linen, white and clean.

This scene is referred to by the Lord Jesus as he describes his coming with *hagios*, or saintly, angels.

> **Mark 8:38** Whosoever therefore shall be ashamed of me and of my words in this adulterous and sinful generation; of him also shall the Son of man be ashamed, when he cometh in the glory of his Father with the holy angels.

ACQUIRING SAINTLY ROBES

Isaiah prophesied of righteous attire in Chapters 61 and 62 of his writing.

> **Isaiah 61:10-11** I will greatly rejoice in the Lord, my soul shall be joyful in my God; for he hath clothed me with the garments of salvation, he hath covered me with the robe of righteousness, as a bridegroom decketh himself with ornaments, and as a bride adorneth herself with her jewels. 11 For as the earth bringeth forth her bud, and as the garden causeth the things

that are sown in it to spring forth; so the Lord God will cause righteousness and praise to spring forth before all the nations.

Isaiah 62:1-3 For Zion's sake will I not hold my peace, and for Jerusalem's sake I will not rest, until the righteousness thereof go forth as brightness, and the salvation thereof as a lamp that burneth. 2 And the Gentiles shall see thy righteousness, and all kings thy glory: and thou shalt be called by a new name, which the mouth of the Lord shall name. 3 Thou shalt also be a crown of glory in the hand of the Lord, and a royal diadem in the hand of thy God.

God is serious about these garments. They are identifying uniforms, but they embody much more than mere visual identity. Power and authority are embodied within this clothing.

Zechariah 3:3-5 Now Joshua was clothed with filthy garments, and stood before the angel. 4 And he answered and spake unto those that stood before him, saying, Take away the filthy garments from him. And unto him he said, Behold, I have caused thine iniquity to pass from thee, and I will clothe thee with change of raiment. 5 And I said, Let them set a fair mitre upon his head. So they set a fair mitre upon his head, and clothed him with garments. And the angel of the Lord stood by.

Joshua was entrusted with a saintly duty during his life, and God outfitted him accordingly. Note once again the accompanying of the angel of the Lord for this righteous duty. As you more fully consider the context of this passage, you will continually see interaction with the angelic. Like a modern day Joshua, God is outfitting the saint in order to do holy bidding in the very face of the enemy.

The enemy will attempt to discredit or pollute the priestly garments of the saints. Before he was commissioned of the Lord, Joshua stood in filthy garments in the presence of demonic opposition. In the final book of the Bible, there is direct opposition between righteous, holy apparel and unrighteous filthy garments.

> **Revelation 22:11** He that is unjust, let him be unjust still: and he which is filthy, let him be filthy still: and he that is righteous, let him be righteous still: and he that is holy, let him be holy still.

It is very clear that if the saint is going to be useful to God, he must remain clean and pure in his spiritual clothing, as attire represents purpose and devotion. It is a church that is holy, or saintly, and without blemish that the Lord is coming to receive.

A grievous error was committed in the translation of the King James Version, and it is found three verses earlier in Revelation 22.

> **Revelation 22:14 Blessed are they that do his commandments**, that they may have right to the tree of life, and may enter in through the gates into the city.

The bolded sequence of this verse, while true, is not even a close translation of the original. In the Greek manuscripts, this literally says that "those who keep their robes clean and washed" will be blessed and will have authority to eat of the tree of life with access into the gates of the city.

It is the responsibility of the saints to watch carefully the condition of their robes. Why this translation error occurred is not really the issue here. The main factor is that we discover the importance of keeping close watch upon the condition of our garments.

> **Ephesians 5:27** That he might present it to himself a glorious church, not having spot, or wrinkle, or any such thing; but that it should be holy and without blemish.

WRINKLES AND SPOTS

These designations are more than poetic expression, as they are very real elements in the spirit realm. Now and then the Lord has opened my eyes to see this phenomenon in action. In my opinion wrinkles represent a double entendre, or competing motive; and spots are active pollutants that must be cleansed.

When my church began to move more closely toward the purposes of God, I could perceive the tangible presence of the Lord on many of our people. Invariably the enemy could see this also and began to work against them. When the enemy infiltrated, some of them began to entertain mixed motives as to what God had called them to be and do. I could see a very real black line that would vertically stretch across the fabric of their composition much like a wrinkle. After a short while, they would fall away from the body unable to be redeemed.

In the natural, wrinkles appear on clothing for a number of reasons. A man wearing a pressed shirt will quickly develop wrinkles if he rests against something or if he engages in some type of physical labor that demands exertion. Just as it is in the natural, should a wrinkle develop, heat and pressure must be applied in order to iron it out. The remedy for wrinkles is commitment to purpose as well as devotion to continue to progress forward.

Spots comprise a very different matter entirely. Where there has been a grievous infringement of enemy doctrine or purpose, a spot will occur. The only remedy is the blood of Jesus. The effects of dealing with a vile and offensive enemy can also soil our conscience. The sprinkling of the blood of Christ, like a purging of hyssop, can affect the strategic areas in which we have been tinged.

Hebrews 9:14 How much more shall the blood of Christ, who through the eternal Spirit offered himself without spot to God, purge your conscience from dead works to serve the living God?

Our wholehearted devotion to our purpose in God and the ongoing empowerment and cleansing of the Blood of Christ will yield our ultimate victory. No matter where the attack may originate or how it might be conducted against us, if we remain true to His purpose and continue to allow for the cleansing of His blood, we cannot be defeated.

> **Revelation 12:11** And they overcame him by the blood of the Lamb, and by the word of their testimony; and they loved not their lives unto the death.

SPOTS AND THE ENEMIES OF RIGHTEOUSNESS

In the following two passages we find accounts that are amazingly similar in detail. Within them the activities of the enemies of righteousness are detailed. Note the time that spots and blemishes come into play.

> **2 Peter 2:13-15** And shall receive the reward of unrighteousness, as they that count it pleasure to riot in the daytime. Spots they are and blemishes, sporting themselves with their own deceivings while they feast with you; 14 Having eyes full of adultery, and that cannot cease from sin; beguiling unstable souls: an heart they have exercised with covetous practices; cursed children: 15 Which have forsaken the right way,

and are gone astray, following the way of Balaam the son of Bosor, who loved the wages of unrighteousness;

Jude 12-13 These are spots in your feasts of charity, when they feast with you, feeding themselves without fear: clouds they are without water, carried about of winds; trees whose fruit withereth, without fruit, twice dead, plucked up by the roots; 13 Raging waves of the sea, foaming out their own shame; wandering stars, to whom is reserved the blackness of darkness for ever.

An important reality for us to consider is that God tells us that there will be many operatives of the enemy that will attempt to infiltrate the places of the people of God. The Bible warns of wolves that will come in sheep's clothing to attempt to ravage the people of God.

A feast of charity is a place where God pours His grace and devotion into a faithful and devoted people. Purpose is directed and equipped. Often the enemy will infiltrate for the goal of discovering the revelation of the ongoing plan of God. If the enemy cannot stop worship, why not join what he cannot prevent?

It is important that we are wise and harmless at the same time. We must trust but be sober and vigilant as our adversary, the enemy, is always on the prowl for what he can devour. A feast of charity is a prime feasting spot.

Further, a consideration of the importance of with whom we fellowship is of utmost consequence. David knew a lot about the heart of God and how a human can be pleasing in His sight. In the very first verse of the introductory chapter of the Book of Psalms, David warns about unwise fellowship.

> **Psalm 1:1** Blessed is the man that walketh not in the counsel of the ungodly, nor standeth in the way of sinners, nor sitteth in the seat of the scornful.

Worshipping the Lord requires diligence in protecting our social environment. Walking, standing and sitting defines the activities in which we need to be careful. The innocent and "harmless" things can prove disastrous to our saintly garments.

WEDDING ATTIRE

It is fitting that we return to the keynote passage in this chapter that concerns the linen of the saints, as the event at which their righteous attire is defined is a marriage feast.

> **Revelation 19:8-9** And to her was granted that she should be arrayed in fine linen, clean and white: for the fine linen is the righteousness of saints. 9 And he saith unto me, Write, Blessed are they which are called unto the marriage supper of the Lamb. And he saith unto me, These are the true sayings of God.

We are currently being bidden to this feast, and it is clear from the following passage that many others are also included on the list of those who will attend.

> **Matthew 22:8-14** Then saith he to his servants, The wedding is ready, but they which were bidden were not worthy. 9 Go ye therefore into the highways, and as many as ye shall find, bid to the marriage. 10 So those servants went out into the highways, and gathered together all as many as they found, both bad and good: and the wedding was furnished with guests. 11 And when the king came in to see the guests, he saw there a man which had not on a wedding garment: 12 And he saith unto him, Friend, how camest thou in hither not having a wedding garment? And he was speechless. 13 Then said the king to the servants, Bind him hand and foot, and take him away, and cast him into outer darkness; there shall be weeping and gnashing of teeth. 14 For many are called, but few are chosen.

The servants extending the invitation are the linen-clad angels of the Lord. Note in Verse 10 that individuals with both good and bad intentions will be bidden to attend this climactic event. These invitations are being issued at this very time. God is actively pursuing the lost and the deceived. He is granting them every opportunity to turn their hearts and giftings to Him.

It is absolutely essential that we place our highest priority upon maintaining our relationship with the Father. The mark of acceptability at this feast is the presence of the wedding garment, which is indicative of the linen of saintly calling and devotion. Giftings and anointings apart from the mandate of righteousness are not enough to qualify for acceptance at this feast of power.

The Saints

Remembering The Love Of The Father

Considering all of the dimensions of development and service, only one factor makes everything else function. No matter how thrilling or challenging the tasks that are to come, one compelling virtue stands as the pinnacle of existence. Of all the things that have been spoken in this book, there is only one essential. That essential, that virtuous factor, is love for our Heavenly Father. Although Jesus loved the world that He was sent to save, He was only able to endure the cross because of His love for the Father.

> **John 14:31** But that the world may know that I love the Father; and as the Father gave me commandment, even so I do. Arise, let us go hence.

Other types of love are powerful, but there is no love to compare with that which is offered to God. Without a loving relationship with our Heavenly Father, there will be no fulfillment, no service and no lasting victory. The Father's love will not only motivate us but will also secure us in our every movement.

PRIME DIRECTIVE

There is a passage of scripture that is too often relegated to weddings and funerals. It is cited as one of the most prolific literary offerings of all time. Of course, I speak of 1 Corinthians 13. This is more than simply a sweet and moving sentiment. It is virtually an index for the saint.

1 Corinthians 12 speaks of gifts of the Spirit. It concludes with the manner in which the grace gifts flow in excellence.

> **1 Corinthians 12:31** But covet earnestly the best gifts: and yet shew I unto you a more excellent way.

This verse does not say that the gifts of the Spirit will be replaced by love. It says that the way the gifts will flow in might and excellence is through something called *agape*. **Charity** is translated from the Greek word *agape*. This is the love of God. Although *agape* will manifest in physical service to others and will grant our minds an appreciation of the beauty of God, *agape's* essence is spiritual. When we say we have *agape,* we are talking about a sacred relationship with God Almighty that transcends all known forms and dimensions of love on earth.

WHAT *AGAPE* IS NOT

> **1 Corinthians 13:1-3** Though I speak with the tongues of men and of angels, and have not charity, I am become as sounding brass, or a tinkling cymbal. 2 And though I have the gift of prophecy, and understand all mysteries, and all knowledge; and though I have all faith, so that I could remove mountains, and have not charity, I am nothing. 3 And though I bestow all my

goods to feed the poor, and though I give my body to be burned, and have not charity, it profiteth me nothing.

In the above progression, speaking with the tongues of men and angels is divers intercession. This is spirit realm communication. Prophecy, revelation of mysteries, and mountain-moving faith is a power progression that the saints will discover. This is a girding of our mind to understand and obey. Sacrificing all of our treasure for the poor and yielding our body as a burning sacrifice is the ultimate of physical devotion and commitment.

When we follow the flow, we find that praying in divers tongues will yield prophetic insight of our purpose in the Lord's service. Submitting ourselves to this purpose will cost us all that we are and possess. All three of these tremendous sacrifices are not *agape* in themselves.

WHAT *AGAPE* INVOLVES

1 Corinthians 13:4-8 Charity suffereth long, and is kind; charity envieth not; charity vaunteth not itself, is not puffed up, 5 doth not behave itself unseemly, seeketh not her own, is not easily provoked, thinketh no evil; 6 Rejoiceth not in iniquity, but rejoiceth in the truth; 7 Beareth all things, believeth all things, hopeth all things, endureth all things. 8 Charity never faileth...

Whenever you are pursuing the *agape* of God, you will labor to rid yourselves of the following: impatience, self, jealousy, pride, self-promotion, aimlessness, envy, anger, lust, iniquity, and unrighteousness.

The *agape* of God will ingrain in you patience and longsuffering, faith, hope, endurance, and the power of the overcoming God.

AGAPE IS ALL THAT MATTERS

> **1 Corinthians 13:8-11** Charity never faileth: but whether there be prophecies, they shall fail; whether there be tongues, they shall cease; whether there be knowledge, it shall vanish away. 9 For we know in part, and we prophesy in part. 10 But when that which is perfect is come, then that which is in part shall be done away. 11 When I was a child, I spake as a child, I understood as a child, I thought as a child: but when I became a man, I put away childish things

Agape does a maturing work within you. Service to the Lord is not about the manifestation of power and revelation of explosive truths. These things will be a part of your experience, but they are only temporary. Becoming a dependable and trusted joint-heir with God will require a purging of immaturity from your life.

Remember that the root word for **saint** is ***hagios***, or holy. The Holy Spirit is literally a saintly wind. A saint is a person who has committed him or herself in order to be changed into the image of God and filled with His fullness and purposes.

A SOBERING CONCLUSION

We conclude our consideration of the saints with a reflection on the challenge of the Ephesians. Perhaps no other community within the early church was as soundly instructed in the things of the spirit realm. An examination of Paul's epistle to the church reveals a depth of understanding that was absolutely phenomenal in scope. Undoubtedly they were in a position of great revelatory import because they were regularly before the Father and firmly established in their seat in the heavenlies. Yet, the Lord Jesus speaks a strong word of warning to them, and it is a word that applies to anyone flowing in the deeper things of the Lord.

> **Revelation 2:4** Nevertheless I have somewhat against thee, because thou hast left thy first love.

No matter how much the Ephesians knew about the things of God, without *agape* they were not acceptable. Regardless of how vital their ministry, love had dissipated.

The Lord commended them for many valuable services to Him, but without a passion for God they were lost. Let this never be said of any of us. You might say that you will never lose your love for the Lord. Think again. As powerful as this gift is, it is only as strong as your commitment to your commune with God.

Life is a funny thing. We seek after what we deem necessary or desirable. When we attain to that acquisition, the thrill often dies. Human nature has a hard time being full and hungry at the same time. Jesus said that we need to learn to be both.

> **Matthew 5:6** Blessed are they which do hunger and thirst after righteousness: for they shall be filled.

We must ask our Father to continually keep the flame of *agape* alive within our heart. Jesus gave the remedy to the Ephesians.

> **Revelation 2:5** Remember therefore from whence thou art fallen, and repent, and do the first works;

Remember. What a simple word yet ripe with meaning. You can fall from a place of great fulfillment. The remedy is in always remembering what brought you to love. What were the first works that established meaning? What were the first expressions of devotion? Remember and do them. Do not ever let them go.

Repent means to turn again. Have other things taken the place of your first love?

Sometimes the things that are birthed through *agape* will take the place of *agape* itself. Apparently that was the case with Ephesus. They were dwelling in established ministry but loveless emotion.

God has called His saints into a walk of pure passion. Responsibilities will come, and they will vie for your attentions. Do the impossible. Seek and find at the same time. Hunger and thirst at the same time. Be weak and strong at the same time. Die and live.

Saints of God ARISE!!! The King of Saints is calling your name.

PNEUMATIKOS PUBLISHING
P.O. Box 595351
Dallas, Texas 75359
(214) 821-5290 fax (214) 821-6760
www.pneumatikos.com or email info@pneumatikos.com

BOOKS YOU NEED TO READ!!

Divers Tongues **By Ronald W. Crawford**
The author, a seasoned pastor, takes us through God's Word as he unveils the strategic communication tool of divers tongues. This long hidden and misunderstood gifting brings spiritual warfare victories that are both wondrous and compelling.

The Pneumatikos **By Ronald W. Crawford**
As Priest of the Most High, the Pneumatikos minister before the very Throne of God. It is their privilege to communicate the secrets of the Kingdom to a church that is hungry for more of God. These spiritual ones are the Kings and Priests of the Book of Revelation, and will proclaim the mysteries of God to this world

Princes of the Dark Realm **By Ronald W. Crawford**
Our enemy is Satan, but he does not fight alone. The Bible directly identifies many evil rulers with which the church must contend, each with very specific tactics and purposes within the kingdom of darkness. The author describes several of these beings from the vantage point of the Word of God, as well as from direct encounters with them. Let us not be ignorant of any of the devices of our enemies. (Coming Soon)

Ministering with Angels **By Paul David Harrison**
One of the distinguishing characteristics of the culminating events in God's timetable will be the influx of the angelic in our churches and individual lives. They are coming at God's bidding to impart gifts and anointings reserved for these last days

Ministering from our Heavenly Seats **By Paul David Harrison**
Scripture says God has "...made us sit together in heavenly places in Christ Jesus". The author describes what it is really like to pray and minister from the seats of authority God has purposed and prepared for His Son's bride, the church. (Coming Soon)

Breaking Chains of Darkness **By Charles Baker, PhD.**
A career engineer and college professor takes you on a 30-year odyssey and Bible study, showing how he got into deliverance ministry and how any Spirit-filled Christian can expel demons, break spoken curses, and end generational curses. Of particular interest is his scriptural explanation of how tactics of the enemy can establish strongholds in Christians and how they be ended by the power of the Blood of Jesus.

ORDER FORM

Books	# of Books	Price Each	Total Cost
Ministering with Angels By Paul David Harrison (Also in Spanish)		10.00	
Divers Tongues By Ronald Crawford		10.00	
Divers Tongues Self-Study Course (need book to complete)		10.00	
Ministering from our Heavenly Seats By Paul David Harrison	COMING SOON		
The Saints By Ronald Crawford		10.00	
Pneumatikos By Ronald Crawford		10.00	
Princes of the Dark Realm By Ronald Crawford	COMING SOON		
Breaking Chains of Darkness By Charles Baker, PhD.		10.00	

Please make checks payable to:

Pneumatikos Publishing
P.O. Box 595351
Dallas, Texas 75359
(214) 821-5290

Sub Total		
Sales Tax 8.25% (Texas Residents only)		
Shipping		
Total		

Shipping		
1 book	add $2.00	
2 -5 books	add $3.00	
6-14 books	add $5.00	
15-25 books	add $7.00	
26 books or more	add 6%	

No COD's
No charge cards
All foreign orders please triple shipping charges

Name: _____

Street or P.O. Box: _____

City: _____ State: _____ Zip Code: _____

Country: _____

Phone Number: _____